THE TREATMENT OF THE CAPITAL SINS AND THE DECALOGUE IN THE GERMAN SERMONS
OF
BERTHOLD VON REGENSBURG

THE CATHOLIC UNIVERSITY OF AMERICA
STUDIES IN GERMAN
VOL. XVII

The Treatment of the Capital Sins and the Decalogue in the German Sermons of Berthold von Regensburg

BY

REMO JOSEPH IANNUCCI

AMS PRESS
NEW YORK

DEDICATED
IN
LOVE AND REVERENCE
TO
THE MEMORY OF MY MOTHER
AND
MY NIECE

ACKNOWLEDGMENTS

The author expresses his sincere gratitude to his father for the opportunity of pursuing graduate studies at the Catholic University of America. He is deeply grateful to Doctor Leo Behrendt, Associate Professor of German, for his kindly encouragement and patient effort which he gave to the direction of this dissertation; to Doctor Paul G. Gleis, Head of the German Department of the Catholic University, for generous, valuable aid offered; and to the Reverend Doctor George B. Stratemeier, O. P., for the reading of the manuscript and constructive criticism. Acknowledgment is also made to the Reverend Doctor Edgar A. Lang, O. S. B., for his invaluable assistance in preparing the manuscript; to the Reverend Charles G. Fehrenbach, C. SS. R., for helpful suggestions. The writer acknowledges also the courteous assistance rendered him by the respective Staffs of the Catholic University Library, and Harvard University Library.

TABLE OF CONTENTS

CHAPTER III

FOREWORD

Medieval concepts of ethics and morals have often attracted the attention of both the theologian and the student of literature, particularly when they are found in sources which reflect popular habits of thought and actions within an important era. The didactic, thirteenth century sermons of Berthold von Regensburg record and indicate many of these ethical elements, and popular superstitions, beliefs, and attitudes, which are valuable from a cultural and historical point of view and which may be represented, classified and analysed through projections of the theological categories such as selected for this study.

Berthold's productivity flourished during times of transition. The century in which he lived and preached witnessed the gradual rise of the middle class, the slow extinction of serfdom, the influence of merchant and artisan, and the increased use of mone-. Neither the lord nor the serf was satisfied with the ancient orde' of things. The serfs began to obtain money by the sale of their products in urban markets. The proprietors found it to their advantage to accept money in place of services. With the increase of trade came the longing of the lower classes for freedom. Towns became more prominent and received charters limiting the rights of the lords. The miller, the blacksmith, the peasant gradually assumed a more important position beside the lord and feudal master.[1a]

Berthold's age was, however, also an age of faith. It was an era which saw great manifestations of religious fervor and pageantry; it was the age of saints. Public penances, long and painful pilgrimages, foundations of cloisters, conversions, also were proofs for that active faith which permeated the people of the thirteenth century. They lived in a supernatural atmosphere: everything that happened was by a supernatural intervention of God, and they continually looked to Him to perform miracles; the " Gottesur-

---

[1a] J. H. Robinson: *An Introduction to the story of Western Europe* (Boston and London, 1903), p. 236.

xi

teile " are an example to the point. The influence of the Church in temporal, and her supremacy in religious matters was a fact which could only strengthen the faith in the supernatural. The pontifical throne had reached the climax of its power. Constantinople itself had become a Latin kingdom, and a Latin church had even been established within its walls.

The time, however, was not without its evils. This young people, full of faith, had many faults. The evils against which Berthold preached are even reflected in the acts of the Council of the Lateran. The records of this Council reveal the presence of corruption in the ranks of the clergy; celibacy was not faithfully adhered to; simony was still prevalent, and many clerics entirely neglected one of the essential duties of their office: the preaching and the teaching of the word of God. Many monasteries had become rich. With opulence, corruption had too frequently entered the sacred inclosure. Among the people was found the strangest mixture of faith and vice. Not only were there great saints and great criminals, but often an individual passed suddenly from sin to self-denial, or from virtue to vice. For the knight of the thirteenth century, God and the lady of his heart, devotion and gallantry, charity and revenge, cloister and battlefield, were all objects equally worthy of his ambition.

The common people of Berthold's time understood abstract ideas only by their concrete realizations—they saw rather than understood. Religion for them consisted in devotions to saints and martyrs, to the person of Christ in the crib or on the cross, and it was mostly unaccompanied by systematic contemplation of great spiritual truths.

Conditions in towns deserve attention, for it was in towns that Berthold's activity mostly exercised itself, and towns represented the rising element of the age. Owing chiefly to the revival of trade at the time of the Crusades, towns had developed rapidly in the twelfth and thirteenth centuries. A mixed population had flocked there. The towns were often the refuge of suspicious characters, of tramps, of beggars, and of criminals who found there a comparatively safe hiding-place. Nobles, too, had gathered to those centers of trade and commerce. Towns were also the seat of much misery; the poor, the infirm, the aged naturally frequented the places where wealth abounded. The misery was further increased by the diseases which then infested the towns. Whatever may have been the political aspect of the social condition, the problem itself was regarded as religious, the evil was considered from a religious point of view, and the remedies offered were religious.

Religion was the basis of everything in the thirteenth century, and everything was seen through a religious coloring. The people were imbued with a great religious spirit. They could never have thought of a political or economic question which was not, before all, a religious question. They did not isolate the political and economic phases of a social system. They saw only lords, serfs, clerics, monks—all more or less in need of religious virtues which might have restored to all peace and happiness. Hence the remedies offered for the failings of the thirteenth century were religious, and all plans of reform were inspired by religion.[1b]

An examination of the bibliography on Berthold von Regensburg reveals the absence of a detailed description, in any separate study, of the ethical and moral material and the background against which this dissertation is projected. Nor has any other work followed the same limited line of research on the treatment of the Capital Sins and the Decalogue in Berthold's sermons. With a view to a definite rather than a broad study of the available material on the subject, the source used for this investigation has been limited to the German sermons which Berthold preached to his vast congregations. The material and citations are based on the Pfeiffer-Strobl edition of *Berthold von Regensburg Predigten*. The writer has given in paraphrase his own translation of the passages selected, and in many cases original quotations, some of greater, some of

---

[1b] Cf. C. T. Rapp, *Burgher and Peasant in the Works of Thomasin von Zirclaria, Freidank, and Hugo von Trimberg*, Diss. (Washington, 1936), vii; L. Dubois, S. M., *Saint Francis of Assisi Social Reformer*, Diss. (Washington, 1904), 9 ff.; K. Unkel, *Berthold von Regensburg* (Köln, 1882), 1 ff.; G. Grupp, *System und Geschichte der Kultur* (Paderborn, 1892), II, 231 ff.

lesser importance, have been supplanted for the sake of complete-
ness, and to give a documented presentation of the preacher's own
views, pictorial diction and method of expression. In few instances
where information was rather scant, references to treatments have
been cited in which a fuller account of the particular subject may
be found.

Sins against the Ten Commandments have been divided into two
separate chapters, the basis of the division being Christ's own words
in the Gospel of St. Matthew (Ch. 22, v. 36-40). Cornelius a
Lapide explains Christ's words: " In his duobus mandatis (viz.,
love of God and love of neighbor) universa lex pendet et prophetae "
in the sense that the first three Commandments of the Mosaic table
are specific applications of the general command to love God with
our whole heart, etc., whereas the last seven detail the specific
obligations of the Commandment of love of neighbor.[2] This interpretation has been accepted by the majority of theologians and
exegetes.

Frequent statements occur in current literature on Berthold to
the effect that information concerning Berthold's life is rather
meager. However, the available material on his life is adequate.[3]
Besides the preacher's method of sermonizing,[4] Berthold has been

[2] Cf. Cornelius a Lapide, *Commentarius in Evangelia*, T. I., 236.

[3] Cf. K. Rieder, *Das Leben Bertholds von Regensburg*, Diss. (Freiburg im
Br., 1901); A. Schönbach, " Ueber Leben, Bildung, und Persönlichkeit
Bertholds von Regensburg," Stücke 7, 8, *Studien zur Geschichte der altdeutschen Predigt* (in *Sitzungsberichte der Wiener Akademie*, 154, 155,
1906); K. Unkel, *op. cit.*, 11-33; C. Stromberger, *Berthold von Regensburg der grösste Volksredner des deutschen Mittelalters* (Gütersloh,
1877, 10-17; M. Bihl, " Ein unediertes Leben Bruder Bertholds von Regensburg," in *Historisches Jahrbuch*, 29 (1908), 590 ff.; F. Pfeiffer, *Berthold
von Regensburg-Predigten* (Wien, 1862), Einleitung; J. Grimm, in
Kleinere Schriften, Bd. IV (Berlin, 1869), 296 ff.

[4] Cf. K. Unkel, *op. cit.*, 46-64; R. Cruel, *Geschichte der deutschen
Predigt im Mittelalter* (Detmold, 1879), 307-322 *passim*; T. Wieser, *Bruder
Berthold von Regensburg* (Programm Brixen, 1889), 10-19; R. Piffl,
Einiges über Berthold von Regensburg (Programm Prag, 1890), 5 f.; H.
Greeven, *Die Predigtweise des Franziskaner's Berthold von Regensburg*
(Programm Rheydt, 1892); G. Coulton, " A Revivalist of Six Centuries
Ago " in *The North American Review*, CLXXXVI (1907), 274 ff.; E. Nuss-
baum, *Metapher und Gleichnis bei Berthold von Regensburg*, Diss. (Wien,
1902), Ch. I, II, *passim*.

studied for the sociological,[5] pedagogical,[6] and humorous aspects [7] of his sermons, as well as for their language and style.[8] Some studies on this medieval Franciscan preacher dealing with phases of theology [9] are obviously biased or disregard the metaphysical foundation of Christian teaching, or lack a systematic, consistent procedure.

Despite the title given his essay *Zur Theologie des Berthold von*

[5] Cf. H. Gildemeister, *Das deutsche Volksleben im XIII. Jahrhundert nach den deutschen Predigten*, Diss. (Jena, 1889). The same material is also found in T. Gärtner's work: *Berthold von Regensburg über die Zustände des deutschen Volks im 13. Jahrhundert* (Programm Zittau, 1890). K. Unkel, *op. cit.*, 64-80; G. Coulton, *loc. cit.*, 276 ff.; E. Nussbaum, *op. cit.*, 44-62; A. Sokol, " Das Grundproblem der Gesellschaft im Spiegel Bertholds von Regensburg," in *The Germanic Review*, XI (1936), 147-163; T. Paul, *Berthold von Regensburg und das bürgerliche Leben seiner Zeit* (Programm Wien, 1896); M. Kohn, " Berthold von Regensburg ein Sozialethiker des Mittelalters," in Wochenschrift *Deutschland*, Nr. 26-28 (1890). E. G. Gudde, " Social Conflicts in Medieval German Poetry," in *Univ. of California Publications in Modern Philology*, Vol. 18 (Univ. of Calif. Press), Berkeley, Calif., 1939. (Gudde refers to Berthold von Regensburg seven times.)

[6] Cf. M. Scheinert, *Der Franziskaner Berthold von Regensburg als Lehrer und Erzieher des Volkes*, Diss. (Leipzig, 1896); E. Michael, *Geschichte des deutschen Volkes vom dreizehnten Jahrhundert bis zum Ausgang des Mittelalters* (Freiburg im Br., 1889), II, 342-347; K. Unkel, *op. cit.*, 83-89; T. Gärtner, *op. cit.*, 9; E. Keil, *Deutsche Sitte und Sittlichkeit nach den damaligen deutschen Predigern* (Dresden, 1931), 110 ff.

[7] Cf. R. Schleich, *Der Humor in den Predigten Bertholds von Regensburg* (Programm Weisskirchen, 1892); R. Pfiffl, *op. cit.*, 31; M. Scheinert, *op. cit.*, 34.

[8] Cf. H. Roetteken, " Der zusammengesetzte Satz bei Berthold von Regensburg," in *Quellen und Forschungen zur Sprach- und Kulturgeschichte der germanischen Völker*, 53 (1885); O. Toifel, *Ueber einige besondere Arten der Satzstellung bei Berthold von Regensburg* (Programm Ried, 1900-01); H. Fassbender, *Die Stellung des Verbums in den Predigten des Berthold von Regensburg*, Diss. (Bonn, 1908); J. Kjederqvist, *Untersuch. über den Gebrauch des Konjunktivs bei Berthold von Regensburg* (Lund, 1896); Scheinert, *op. cit.*, 22 ff.; Grimm, *op. cit.*, 347 ff.

[9] Cf. K. Föste, *Zur Theologie des Berthold von Regensburg* (Programm Zwickau, 1890); E. Keil, *op. cit.*; O. Koch, *Die Bibelzitate in den Predigten Bertholds von Regensburg*, Diss. (Greifswald, 1909); A. Lebsanft, *Die religiösen und ethischen Ausdrücke bei Berthold von Regensburg*, Diss. (Tübingen, 1923); E. Bernhardt, *Bruder Berthold von Regensburg* (Erfurt, 1905), treats also the cultural aspects.

Regensburg, Karl Föste offers only a meandering representation of
Berthold's moral and dogmatic theology. In his simple, unsatis-
factory outline, the capital sins, for example, are merely referred to
casually as a minor subdivision of actual sins which are divided into
two classes: mortal sins, and venial sins. He dismisses the subject with the phrase: " Berthold weiss, daß die Zahl der Todsünden
gewöhnlich auf sieben angegeben wird . . . " and simply names the
sins without comment.[10] On page 16 f. he properly presents Love
and Hope as second and third theological virtues which he calls
cardinal virtues. Faith, the primary theological virtue, is not mentioned. However, on page 13 f. two very brief paragraphs are given
on Faith which are far removed from the real and complete picture
as found in the sermons. No mention of the decalogue is made
throughout the entire treatise.

Ernst Keil called his more elaborate work " Customs and Morality
of the Thirteenth Century according to the Preachers of that
Period." This is at best a misleading title. The whole study,
almost completely devoid of comment and paraphrase, seems concerned only with Berthold. Very few and only casual quotations
from other sermons found in Grieshaber's and Schönbach's collec-
tions occur in Keil's dissertation. He does not treat the capital
sins and decalogue as such. Besides, his work emphasizes only the
sociological consequences of transgressions in one or the other Commandment rather than the heinous offences against God—the light
in which Berthold always saw and preached against these transgressions. It is more a sociological study than one in the history
of ethical outlook and method. The author treats *luxuria* and
adultery, for instance, from purely secular and social viewpoints:
the former is the vice that jeopardizes family life; the latter is
merely a sin against married life, and, apparently, not against the
sixth Commandment.

Another consideration makes the study of Berthold's ethics de-
sirable. Erich Aumann recently wrote an article " Tugend und
Laster im Althochdeutschen." He describes four meanings for
tugent in early times. Aumann's conclusions may be tested and
complimented in this study in the light of an investigation of Berthold's concepts of virtue and vice. Berthold's treatment of morality

[10] Cf. K. Föste, *op. cit.,* 7 f.

may also, in passing, be compared with that of some of his contemporaries, predecessors, and successors after a systematic presentation of Berthold's concept of the scope of sins as attempted in this study. The ethical teachings of Hugo von Trimberg, Thomasin von Zirclaria, Freidank, Winsbeke and others have already been studied by some scholars in that field. The moral outlook of German Christian writers in the twelfth and thirteenth centuries has recently been discussed again by scholars like G. Weber, G. Ehrismann, H. Schneider, J. Bühler, G. Rosenhagen, E. Wechsler, J. Huizinga, M. Hermann, A. von Martin, E. Troeltsch, especially in connection with present-day ideology in certain European countries. Terms and fundamental information, however, are by no means clear or comprehensive. The history of the treatment of capital sins has been studied many years ago by S. Stone, and P. Schulze, and the decalogue by D. Meisner, G. Robinson, and L. Lemme. Marriage, and the place of woman in the Middle Ages are again topics of scientific dispute. The medieval Church is accused of a strongly negative, ascetic attitude toward problems of life. We may ask ourselves furthermore, " Can Berthold—as is so often claimed—be considered a forerunner of the Protestant Reformation as far as some of his views are concerned ? " The object of this dissertation, then, will be to examine the German sermons of Berthold for the evidence which they contain on the moral life of the times and the moral concepts of Berthold. The search is directed especially toward those details and concrete items of the sermons which are not regularly included in the special histories and which have not been exhaustively or systematically treated by others. It is hoped that the present study may clarify our notions somewhat on the moral conditions of the thirteenth century and Berthold's moral views. It will, of course, not be forgotten that the preacher exaggerated considerably, and that a careful appraisal is necessary to arrive at correct general conclusions.

CHAPTER I

THE CAPITAL SINS AND THEIR CORRESPONDING VIRTUES

The thirteenth century in Germany was a period of marked religious, moral, political, social, and economic transitions. The writers and preachers of the times, therefore, often took a definite stand regarding the new developments in the " kaiserlose, schreckliche Zeit." Their works naturally often mirror their personal reactions to the new order.[1] The exhortations of Berthold von Regensburg, like those of his contemporary Hugo von Trimberg (in Hugo's extensive poetic work the *Renner*) frequently represent a popular elaboration of the moral teaching of the Christian Church applied to conditions of their age. The fact that they are based in a large part on the doctrine of the seven capital sins apparently reflects an important phase of the moral conditions of the times and also the moral system as known to the thirteenth century.[2]

The seven capital sins have always had a prominent place in Treatises on Christian spiritual life, and literature.[3] Cassian (360-435) treats of them at length in his *Conferences* and *Institutes*.[4] He enumerates eight instead of seven because he separates pride from vain-glory. St. Gregory the Great (540-604) clearly distinguishes the seven capital sins, all of which he traces to pride.[5] St. Thomas Aquinas (1225-1274) also derives them [6] all from pride and shows how they can be logically classified, if account is taken

---

[1] Cf. M. P. Goetz, *The Concept of Nobility in German Didactic Literature of the Thirteenth Century*, Diss. (Washington, 1935), v.

[2] Cf. L. Behrendt, *The Ethical Teaching of Hugo von Trimberg*, Diss. (Washington, 1926), 12.

[3] Cf. A. Tanquerey, *Précis de Théologie Ascétique et Mystique* (Paris, 1924), II, 524.

[4] Cf. *De institutis coenobiorum et de octo principalium vitiorum* . . . , ed. by M. Petschenig (Vienna, 1888).

[5] Cf. *Moral.*, I. xxxl, c. XLV.

[6] Cf. *Summa Theologiae*, Ia IIae, q. 84, a. 3, a. 4. IIa IIae, q. 31, a. 5; q. 35, a. 4; q. 118, a. 7, a. 8; q. 148, a. 5; q. 153, a. 4; q. 158, a. 6. IIa IIae, q. 55, a. 4. IIa IIae, q. 34, a. 5.

1

of the *special ends* toward which man is drawn. For many centuries moralists groped their way toward a classification of the
deadly or capital sins that would be final in number, names and
arrangement.[7] Approximately in the year 350 A. D. the ogdoad
was developed in the Christian monastic life of Egypt and Syria,
an arrangement of the capital sins, which later, 600 A. D., served
Pope Gregory the Great to set on another basis, the heptad.[8]

It is interesting and instructive to study the sermons of Berthold
von Regensburg, which occupy one of the most prominent places in
" geistliche Literatur " of the Middle Ages, in the light of comparison with the moral German poetical literature preceding and
accompanying his own times. Some relevant material to form the
base from which similarities of Berthold's views with, or differences
from earlier writings may be gathered and presented, may be found
in summary fashion in the Zweiter Teil, 1. Frühmittelhochdeutsche
Zeit, of Gustav Ehrismann's *Geschichte der deutschen Literatur bis
zum Ausgang des Mittelalters,* and similar works by Golther, H.
Schneider, Vogt, Kogel, and Schwietering.

With respect to the rather negative approach and extreme rigid-
ness which Berthold employed in his exhortations, the seed of a
definite similarity in method seems to have been planted in the
Cluniac movement as reflected in the work *Memento Mori* (ca.
1070), and in two moralistic poems of Heinrich von Melk (ca.
115ᵒ). It was probably in the former production that the social
element seen through religious eyes, which later Heinrich von
Melk developed more extensively, had its first prominent representative in clerical German poetical literature. For the first time
are clearly pointed out in these works, the moral offences more
frequently committed by different ranks in society. *Memento Mori,*
on a much smaller and less forceful scale than found in Berthold's
sermons, warns the rich to perform good works, and advocates that
the poor be sheltered from injustice. Like Berthold, Heinrich von
Melk even enumerates, although restrictedly, the transgressions
peculiar to certain classes: members of the high class are often
guilty of pride and avarice; priests, of unchastity, gluttony, simony,

[7] Cf. F. Tupper, *Types of Society in Medieval Literature* (New York,
1926), 64.

[8] Cf. Behrendt, *op. cit.,* 54 f.

and avarice; and monks, of " Klostersünden." In almost the same way, too, the offence itself against God does not receive as much attention as does the idea of death. Heinrich von Melk is referred to as " ein schonungsloser Fanatiker " by Ehrismann because Ehrismann claims that he has no mercy or pardon for the individual that has sinned. Berthold, of course, is equally as rigid; however, he does very frequently, after he has figuratively scourged the sinner, insert the statement: " buoze nim ich alle zît ûs." Thus is the contrite person excepted from Berthold's censures.

The poem *Vom Rechte*, like *Memento Mori* and the works of Heinrich von Melk, may also be classified as a sermon. In *Vom Rechte*, too, complaints are registered against oppressors of the poor: unjust judges, and the rich. Among the virtues which Berthold mentions as remedies for oppression, Justice and Love, *Vom Rechte* suggests in addition, Truth.

Several additional monuments of early Middle High German show some marks of similarity in the treatment accorded certain subjects as discussed later by Berthold von Regensburg. An interesting observation can be made, at this point, with regard to the consistent, strong emphasis placed on virtue alone which is found in some of the earliest clerical writings. In direct contrast thereto, virtue in the sermons of Berthold von Regensburg occupies a minor position compared with the vehemence with which sin is always brought to the foreground. Differing from the three aforementioned productions that limit their number of virtues, placing special stress on Justice, *Das St. Trudperter hohe Lied*, for instance, is the one work that embodies *all* the virtues which are mentioned and discussed in Berthold's sermons. Typical of the literature of those times, *das St. Trud. h. Lied* does not present virtues systematically; they appear only at random through the text with no mention of the proper category to which they belong. The Theological Virtues only are mentioned as being three; the greatest of which is Love of God and Neighbor. The " Mother " of all virtues is referred to as *unterschidunge*, i. e., the ability to distinguish between Good and Evil. Berthold does not show preference for any one virtue. To him each virtue is " one of the greatest in the world." Another point of interest imparted in the *Lied* is that perfection may be obtained only through good works and

4   *The German Sermons of Berthold von Regensburg*

mortification of the flesh. Throughout *das St. Trud. h. Lied* the author relies entirely on the Benedictine Rule. Berthold does not mention St. Benedict; on the other hand, he quotes freely from Holy Writ, and St. Augustine.

Several times in his sermons Berthold warns the laity against meditating upon the mysteries of the Christian Faith lest they cultivate doubts and weaken their belief. The same warning takes place in *Das Anegenge* (ca. 1160). Another poem in which a single similarity with Berthold occurs is *Von den zehn Geboten*. In this work, too, the distinction is drawn between the first three Commandements and the remaining seven: the first three pertain to God, the last seven to our neighbor.

Certain discussions in *Die altdeutsche Genesis und Exodus* have almost identical treatment in Berthold's sermons. They seem to agree in purpose (to reform the sinner through true repentance which happens to be also the principal theme of *Babylonische Gefangenschaft*; that everyone should be ever mindful of death, and the salvation of his soul), and tone (direction of thoughts to the masses in simple language). The *Wiener Genesis* frequently introduces the devil who takes souls from this world through lust, pride, avarice, hatred, and envy—*five* capital sins. It seems that heathens, as the exponents of pride, are inveighed against for the first time in the second section of the work, *Exodus* (ca. 1163).

Whatever the similarities may be that exist between earlier religious literature and Berthold's sermons, and whatever may have been Berthold's familiarity with those productions, the conclusion that he was in no way influenced by them may readily be drawn. The dissertation at hand together with other separate studies on Berthold von Regensburg provide sufficient evidence that Berthold can claim the distinction for having no direct predecessor· Because of his originality, his determination, his language and method, Berthold von Regensburg remains the first great, genuine moralist-preacher in the history of German religious literature.

While Berthold's enumeration of the capital sins tallies with the fixed and accepted scheme of St. Gregory, the former frequently disregards both order and classification.[9] However, this is

[9] Cf. K. Föste, *Zur Theologie des Berthold von Regensburg* (Progr. Zwickau, 1890), 8. He says further: "In der sechsten Predigt werden

typical of Berthold and other monastic preachers, e. g., St. Anthony of Padua.[10] In view of this fact one also observes in Berthold's sermons departures from the logical presentation of given subjects,[11] and his ever recurring repetitions are found in a great number of the sermons.[12] Capital " sins " are tendencies as well as sins; they are called *sins*, because they lead to sins; they are termed *capital*, because they are the fountain-head or source from which other sins arise.[13] Just as there is in a soul in the state of grace a definite disposition (*habitus*) which supports virtue, so there is in a soul in the state of sin, a similar *habitus* which acts in the opposite direction, and leads to vice.[14] Although, according to Christian teaching, we are cleansed of original sin in Baptism, that *habitus* towards vice remains and is more firmly established by personal sin; and thus from the inherited *habitus* there originates an acquired *habitus*.[15]

genannt: Neid und Hass, Unkeuschheit, Ueppigkeit, übele Zunge, Untreue, unrechte Gewalt, Vorenthaltung des Lohnes, Mord und Totschlag (*manslaht*), stumme Sünde; zu letzterer vergl. I 92, 20. 206, 34, 279, 30. In der siebenten und dreizehnten Predigt führt er an: Hass und Neid, Zorn, Trägheit zum Gottesdienst, Unmässigkeit (*frâzheit*), Hoffart, Unkeuschheit, Habsucht (*gîtikeit*). In der achten Predigt: Hoffart in der Haartracht bei Geistlichen und Laien, Unkeuschheit, Zungensünden, Hoffart in der Kleidung, Habsucht, Unterstützung der Gottlosen, der Ketzer und der Gebannten, Gewaltthat." 8.

  [10] Cf. J. M. Neale, *Medieval Preachers and Medieval Preaching* (London, 1856), 221. For other similarities to St. Anthony, cf. H. Hefele, *Die Bettelorden und das religiöse Volksleben Ober- Mittelitaliens im XIII. Jahrhundert*, Tübingen Diss. (Leipzig, 1910), 92 ff.

  [11] Cf. R. Cruel, *Geschichte der deutschen Predigt im Mittelalter* (Detmold, 1879), 309. Cf. also K. Unkel, *Berthold von Regensburg* (Köln, 1882), 48.

  [12] Cf. Unkel, *op. cit.*, 34, 50. Unkel analyses several sermons to explain his point: for poor logic, 48; for repetitions, 34.

  [13] Cf. Tanquerey, *op. cit.*

  [14] Cf. F. Götting, *Der Renner Hugo's von Trimberg* (Münster i. W., 1932), 69.

  [15] Cf. *ibid.*; cf. also St. Thomas Aquinas, Ia IIae q. 81, a. 4: "... quod peccatum comparatur ad virtutem, sicut actus malus ad habitum bonum. Aliter autem se habet habitus in anima, et forma in re naturali. Forma enim naturalis ex necessitate producit operationem sibi convenientem; unde non potest esse simul cum forma naturali actus formae contrariae; ... Sed habitus in anima non ex necessitate producit suam operationem, sed

Therefore in the Christian system of morals, sin and virtue are placed in parallel order.[16] Berthold also treats "seven virtues"—in a separate sermon—without, however, opposing them as such to seven capital sins.

Berthold stresses more the significance of vice and crime than that of virtue,[17] owing to the religious and political conditions of the times.[18] His sermons contain, moreover, only the final, *practical* application of moral axioms; the purely *theological* problems of morals he evades entirely.[19] It must be remembered that Berthold directed his sermons to the masses; consequently he ignored an approach which presupposed an intimacy with dogmatic and moral problems. He was, after all, *Volksprediger.* However, this should not convey the impression that he was not versed in theology, Sacred Scripture and other knowledge pertaining to his calling in life; [20] although some writers would have us believe the contrary.[21]

homo utitur eo cum voluerit; unde simul habitu in homine existente, potest non uti habitu, aut agere contrarium actum; et sic potest habens virtutem procedere ad actum peccati. Actus vero peccati si comparetur ad ipsam virtutem, prout est habitus quidam, non potest ipsam corrumpere, si sit unus tantum. Sicut enim non generatur habitus per unum actum, ita nec per unum actum corrumpitur, ut supra dictum est."

[16] Cf. Götting, *op. cit.*, 70.

[17] Cf. Piffl, *Einiges über Berthold von Regensburg* (Progr., Prag, 1890), 28.

[18] Cf. T. Wieser, *Bruder Berthold von Regensburg* (Progr., Brixen, 1889), 1. Cf. also Unkel, *op. cit.*, 1 ff.; T. Gärtner, *Berthold von Regensburg über die Zustände des deutschen Volks im 13. Jahrhundert* (Prog., Zittau, 1890), 17 ff.; and Hamberger, " *Berthold von Regensburg*," in *Allgemeine Deutsche Biographie* (Leipzig, 1875), II, 547.

[19] Hugo von Trimberg's method is the same; cf. Götting, *op. cit.*, 27. Cf. Steinmeyer, " Berthold von Regensburg," in *Realencyklopädie für Protestantische Theologie und Kirche* (Leipzig, 1897), 3. Aufl., II, 651.

[20] A. Schönbach, " Studien zur Geschichte der altdeutschen Predigt," 6tes. Stück, in *Sitzungsberichte der Wiener Akademie* (Wien, 1906), Bd. 153, 48: " Berthold von Regensburg selbst beherrschte die Bibel vollkommen, besass die Fähigkeit, ihre Texte genau anzuführen, und auch die strenge Absicht." P. 49: " Berthold kennt die Bibel in ihrem ganzen Umfange, er schöpft aus allen Büchern und zitiert häufig auch Schriften, die sonst in der mittelalterlichen Predigt sich selten angeführt finden. . . ." Cf. also the dissertation of O. Koch, *Die Bibelzitate in den Predigten Bertholds von Regensburg* (Greifswald, 1909), *passim.*

[21] R. Piffl, *op. cit.*, 19: " . . . Berthold . . . ausgerüstet mit einem leid-

A. PRIDE

In his treatment of the first capital vice, Berthold is principally concerned with the element of demoralization affecting various castes of society and their shortcomings. Women,[22] especially, are flayed for their elaborate raiment [23] because this tempts to pride. As Berthold points out, women were created for heaven as well as men, hence heaven is also their ultimate goal.[24] However, a great number of women might attain heaven were it not for pride.[25] Luxurious apparel, unfortunately, is one of the prime factors which causes a majority of women to succumb to excessive pride and vanity; and this may entail loss of eternal happiness.

. . . ir frouwen . . . sô mit gewande, sô mit vorgange zuo dem opfer, mit ebentiure, mit tüechelehen, mit gelwem gebende, mit sleigern unde mit waehen naeten. Sô naewet ir hie den schilt . . . hie den tôren, dâ den affen . . . hâst dû anders niht danne löbelachen unde hôhvart . . . dâ von kument sie niemer in daz geheizen lant. (1 53, 1 ff.) [26]

Reproaching women further, the preacher says:

Ir habet ouch vil maniger hande hôhvart, der ir wol gerietet und iuch ouch des wâren sunnen irret, daz ir in niemer mêr gesehet. Wan ir wellet iuwer herze niht reine machen vor der hôhvart. . . . Ez ist gar ein niht, dâ mit ir daz himelriche verlieset. . . . Ir gêt niwan mit tüechelehe. . . . Ez ist ein gespöte daz hohvertelîn, . . . dâ ir frouwen mit umbe gêt. (1 387, 3 ff.)

lichen Bibelwissen . . ." The *Enciclopedia Italiana*, VI, 793, mentions: ". . . non si può dire che B. (Bertoldo di Ratisbona) sia stato un erudito teologo."

[22] Cf. Wieser, *op. cit.*, 31 f. For information on medieval women, cf. K. Weinhold, *Die deutschen Frauen in dem Mittelalter* (Gekürzte Ausgabe, H. Weiske, Leipzig, 1930). Cf. also Tupper, *op. cit.*, 107-159; and for a good treatment of medieval attire, cf. M. von Boehn, *Die Mode: Menschen und Moden im Mittelalter* (München, 1925).

[23] Cf. J. Dieffenbacher, *Deutsches Leben im 12. und 13. Jahrhundert* (Berlin, 1918), II, 56-61.

[24] Cf. I 414, 2 ff. [25] Cf. *ibid.*, 5 ff.; II 142, *passim*.

[26] For similar references, cf. I 118, 3 ff., 173, 2 ff., 396, 39 ff.; II 101, 37 ff., 120, 2 ff., 181, 17 f. This is typical of the Franciscan sermon even during the times of St. Bernardine of Siena (1380-1444), who discusses the subject almost indentically as Berthold. Cf. K. Hefele, *Der hl. Bernhardin von Siena und die Franziskanische Wanderpredigt in Italien* (Freiburg im Br., 1912), 43-45; 261-262.

And a later passage in the same vein reads:

Und aber ir frouwen, ir trîbet daz wunder von hôhvart, daz ir iuch sîn
iemer müezet schemen in iuwerm herzen wider got unde wider die werlt,
wan ir tuot ofte selber mit iu, unde taeten ez ander liute, ir kündet ir vil
wol gespotten unde vil dar zuo gereden. . . . Seht, daz ist dâ von, daz
iuch diu hôhvart alse gar erblendet hât. . . .   (1 485, 27 ff.)

Similarly, men do not escape the preacher's censures against
elaborate attire.[27]   They, too, are frequently cautioned to thwart
pride, lest they suffer the loss of their souls.

Ir man, ir trîbet ouch ze vil hôhvart, mit waehen sniten an iuwerm
gewande, mit niuwen sniten an hüeten und an anderm. Die habent der
wîsunge unsers herren niht; dâ von kument sie niemer in daz geheizen
lant.   (1 54, 8 ff.)

Berthold furthermore tells his auditors that persons often become very arrogant through pride;[28] and immediately he levels
additional censures at men on account of their vanity:

. . . ir bedörftet über ein niht sô maniger leie hôhvart unde sô maniges
überigen muotes, des ir iu erdenket, niuwen mit iuwern kleidern, daz iu
des niht genüeget, daz iu der almehtige got sô maniger hande gezierde hât
gegeben, niuwen alleine mit gewande.   (1 395, 26 ff.)

The preacher instructs them that God has lent clothing, like other
things which He created, merely for man's benefit, which he must
not abuse.[29]   Berthold assumes a different tone when he informs
the populace of the *one* time that ornamented apparel may be
tolerated: at church on ecclesiastical feast days.[30]

Only once he briefly mentions priests when speaking of this
vice; he says they allow their hair to grow: *wider reht durch
hôhvart unde durch lôsheit.*[31]   And still on the subject of pride,
he resumes his bitter denouncements against men:

----

[27] A description of men's clothing is given in Dieffenbacher, *op. cit.*, II,
61-64.

[28] Cf. I 395, 25.   [29] Cf. *ibid.*, 31 ff.

[30] Cf. *ibid.*, 35 ff. Berthold says there are times when higher praise and
honor should be offered to Our Lord. And since altars are decorated, and
longer and more beautiful songs are sung on holy feast days, people, therefore, are to bedeck themselves all the more attractively to honor and praise
Almighty God. But they must be on guard against pride while in Church.
Cf. II 252, 33 ff.

[31] Cf. I 114, 20 f.

... alle die als langez hâr tragent als diu wîp, daz sie rehte wîbes herzen tragent als diu wîp und an deheiner stat einen man verstên mügent. Pfî dich, Adelheit, mit dînem langen hâre. ...   (1 114, 28 ff.)

and women:

... ir leget daz jâr wol halbez an iuwer hâr ... die ez dâ sô noetlichen machent ... unde mit dem gebende ... die sie gilwent sam die jüdinne ... unde als pfeffinne: anders nieman sol gelwez gebende tragen.

(1 114, 32 ff.; 115, 1 ff.)

Notwithstanding his obligation to speak at greater length on this topic, Berthold says he wishes to discourse sparingly in regard to this, lest he be guilty of teaching more vanity to a laity already sufficiently familiar with this fault.[32] The speaker asserts, moreover, that pride is *gar und gar* peculiar to the wealthy.[33] The devil has ensnared them by pride and prompted them to believe that they, by mere almsgiving and pilgrimages, might merit eternal happiness.[34] In the sermon *Von vier stricken*, Berthold repeats the topic on clothing, and compares the rich to gay-colored birds because,

die fliegent frîlîche hin unde her unde singent gar schône unde sint alle zît froelîchen unde quotes muotes unde fürhtent niemanne unde sint veizt an dem lîbe unde wol bekleit. ... Sie habent maniger hande kleit unde gar fremediu kleit. ... Ez ist dér wîz, der swarz ... der rot. ...

(1 483, 36 ff.)

After quoting St. Augustine, " diu hôhvart wehset in dem rîchtuome als der made in dem apfel," Berthold warns the rich against victimizing the poor by their arrogant authority which they have usurped through sheer pride.[35]

But even the poor can be guilty of pride by an inordinate desire for honor, esteem and power, while others fall for the sake of their children.[36] A number among the poor are incapable of anything but

daz ez hôhvertic mit rüemen ... unde mit andern lügen ist unde sich rüemet friunde die ez nie niht bestuonden unde seit von grôzer üppigkeit

---

[32] Cf. *ibid.*, 33 ff.
[33] Cf. I 88, 39 f.
[34] Cf. I 483, 27 ff.
[35] Cf. I 484, 6 ff., *ibid.*, 14 f., *ibid.*, 38 f.
[36] Cf. I 104, 23 ff.; 469, 25 ff.

unde von hôhvart . . . unde rüemet sich der hôhvart unde ziuhet·sich daz
an, des ez nie schuldic wart.   Sê, sô ist der tiuvel genuoc gewaltic an dir
worden. . . .   (1 526, 34 ff.)

And, should this be insufficient, they exercise still more pride:

. . . sô rücket ez die gürteln hôher; sô hôhvertet einz von sînem wolsingen
. . . einz von sînem gewande, einz von nihte. . . . Daz ein houbettüechelîn
hât, daz kûme zweier pfenninge wert ist, daz gilwest dû unde machest ez
mit krenzelînen unde mit îtelkeit und eht mit nihte.   (1 527, 9 ff.)

Young people also are included among those often guilty of pride,
because by dressing elaborately they believe to derive pleasure; [37]
because by an air of superiority they hope to make their friends
more accommodating,[38] and also because they think it befits their
youthful sense of freedom.[39]

Dancing, though innocent in itself, may be the cause for the
proud of heart to endanger their souls.[40] Women seem to be pre-
dominant in this category.[41]

Wê, ir frouwen! . . . daz dû begerst mit aller dîner kraft solicher üp-
pikeite . . . daz dû dâ mite verdampt bist als Lucifer. (1 173, 4 f.; 8 ff.)

Sarcastically, Berthold continues his invectives against taking much
pride in dancing:

Pfî, ir îtelmecherin und ir tenzelerin und ir·verwerin, ir arme hôhverti-
gaere! Iuwer dinc ist gar ein gespötte wider der gezierdc unde schônheit,
die her Salomôn hete; . . . Er hete dannoch mêr, daz ze der hôhverte
gezôch: er hete ouch springerinne. . . . Unde . . . hât uns got erzöuget,
daz dû hôhvertiger vil mêr müewe und arbeit hâst mit dîner hôhverte. . . .
Swenne dû verst an einen tanz alle tage als ein hirzler . . . unde soltest
dû daz eine wochen trîben, dû woltest ê an einem galgen hangen.
                                                            (1 176, 10 ff.)

Physical exhaustion in dancing Berthold compares to exhaustion

---

[37] Cf. I 469, 23; I 104, 16 f.
[38] Cf. I 469, 23 f.   [39] Cf. I 104, 17 f.
[40] Cf. I 173, 1 ff. The dance was very popular among the Germans of
the thirteenth century. Cf. C. T. Rapp, *Burgher and Peasant in the Works
of Thomasin von Zirclaria, Freidank, and Hugo von Trimberg*, Diss. (Washington, 1936), 26-29. Cf. also Dieffenbacher, *op. cit.*, II 97-99, and R.
Stork, *Der Tanz* (Sammlung illustrierter Monogr.) (Leipzig, 1903).
[41] Cf. I 173, 2 f.; II 576 f.

at death when heavy breathing that contracts and relaxes the shoulders, may indicate death of the soul, too, if the shoulders and the whole body have frequently borne pride.[42] Thus the soul may struggle in the body that while dancing shakes its shoulders and head, and often twists and bends, and arrogantly displays pride in the dance.[43]

Berthold reminds his hearers that thousands of angels had to retreat from heaven because they disturbed the tranquility of the order they should have kept eternally with God, and, like these fallen angels, Adam was made to quit Paradise because he broke his peace by pride. The proud never have peace.[44]

As a complacent passion or sentiment of self-love, pride, in Christian moral concept, is mostly associated with related qualities of the selfish disposition such as arrogance, conceit, vanity, and egotism. Conceit is considered an exaggerated form of self-satisfaction; arrogance is interpreted as an attitude of presumption and ambition manifested in temper and act and calculated to arouse resentment or disgust in others; vanity, as a showing off of one's egotism is explained to be a habit of self-consciousness or self-regard which affects mind, manner, and speech. Since pride is a habit of self-isolation, a non-subjection to God, the perversity of will undoubtedly causes indifferentism and repudiation of all idea of obligation.[45]

Berthold, it seems, dwells mostly upon luxurious apparel when he inveighs against pride. His treatment, of course, seems inadequate because one would normally expect him to discuss more broadly the vice (pride) to which so many other sins are traceable in addition to those he mentions. However, since principles concerning dress are apparently his major points, it is safe to assume that Berthold, inveighing against what was evidently a popular sin, had the intention to shield people from scandal, uncharitableness, unchastity, and immodesty.

By his very nature, man is subject to sensual appeal. Any action calculated to arouse his passions is, according to the degree of

[42] Cf. I 514, 38 ff.

[43] Cf. I 515, 3 ff.   [44] Cf. I 238, 13 ff.; II 68, 13 ff.

[45] Cf. R. Pope, " Pride," in *Encyclopedia of Religion and Ethics* (New York, 1919), X, 275.

deliberateness involved, more or less sinful. This also holds true of the manner in which a woman dresses. Her dress may be of a character to constitute a sensual appeal. If this is the case, the wearer incurs responsibility for the temptations to which she exposes others, in the measure in which she is aware of the consequence of her action. Improper dress may be the occasion of the sins committed. The wearer, moreover, may lead others to temptation by bad example.

Charity requires that a person safeguard himself or herself against temptation and to assist others in the struggle against sin. Immodest dress is contrary to charity because in itself it is an allurement to sin.

Modesty is a protection against one's sensual nature. It acquires the dignity of a virtue, and safeguards chastity.

It has been observed that according to Berthold, for the most part, the rich fall into the category of false pride in dressing. With the poor, Berthold associates more a desire for honor, esteem, power, and boasting; indirectly, the same is applied to the young. The latter instances may be explained from a psychological point of view: the poor, conscious of their needs and desirous to be on equal level with the rich, may seek an escape for their lack of enjoyment of luxuries, and thus from a feeling of embarrassment, they may commit the sins that originate in pride.

Berthold's invectives against a display of pride as expressed in the dance, also permits of a comment. St. Thomas states (IIa IIae q. 168 a. 2) that an individual's movement and gestures, so far as they are governed by reason, can be ordered by it. This ordering by reason is either according to what is becoming to the individual, or what is fitting with reference to other persons, places, or occasions. Motions and gestures are a sign of the inward disposition; government of these requires government of the inward passions. Furthermore, an individual presents himself in deeds and words such as he inwardly is.

a. *Virtue Opposed to Pride*: *Humility* [46]

The congregation is told by Berthold that the bitterest, hardest, yet speediest road to heaven is martyrdom; [47] that thousands of saints entered this way particularly after the birth of Christ. [48] However, torture is difficult to bear and causes horrible pain, and for this reason many persons became disloyal to the Christian faith. [49] Therefore Our Lord found another road to heaven—the way of Mercy. [50] Nevertheless, as long as the Antichrist reigns, the road to martyrdom will again be opened, and Berthold strictly instructs his auditors not to follow the Antichrist; that they should hide in holes or on the highest mountain, for it is better to suffer torture for a short while than to burn eternally with the devil. [51]

But of course centuries have elapsed since individuals attained heaven by martyrdom, hence everyone must acquaint himself with the three highest virtues with which the world is blessed: [52] Humility, Chastity, Charity. [53] Without the possesion of these virtues no one may enter the Kingdom of Heaven, though he owned all the other virtues proclaimed by the world. [54]

Berthold informs the people that if they do not slough off pride and execute the command of God to adopt humility (*demüetikeit*),

---

[46] Berthold has no definite system in his treatment of virtues. Cf. also Föste, *op. cit.*, 13: "In der siebenten Predigt nennt er sieben Tugenden: Liebe (*minne*), Geduld, Eifer zu allen guten Dingen, besonders zum Gottesdienst, Mässigkeit, Demut, Keuschheit, Wohltätigkeit (*miltekeit*). In der achtzehnten Predigt fügt er diesen noch den Glauben hinzu. In der dreissigsten nennt er Keuschheit, Demut, Wohltätigkeit, Treue; in der vierunddreissigsten: Glaube, Liebe, Hoffnung, Beständigkeit (*staetigkeit*). An einigen Stellen (I 249, 16. 443, 19) redet er sogar von zweiundvierzig Tugenden, die jeder Mensch haben müsse, ohne sie jedoch einzeln anzugeben. Cf. also E. Keil, *Deutsche Sitte und Sittlichkeit im 13. Jahrhundert nach den damaligen deutschen Predigern* (Dresden, 1931), 18 f. For a brief treatment of the virtue of humility, cf. J. Mausbach, *Katholische Moraltheologie* (Münster i. W., 1921), 223-228.

[47] Cf. I 171, 22 ff. Berthold employs still other examples of how to reach heaven: II 154 ff.

[48] Cf. I 172, 2; 171, 19.   [49] Cf. I 171, 26 ff.   [50] Cf. *ibid.*, 38.

[51] Cf. I 172, 6 ff. For Berthold's treatment of the Antichrist, cf. A. Franz, *Drei deutsche Minoritenprediger aus dem XIII. und XIV. Jahrhundert* (Freiburg im Br., 1907), 70 ff.

[52] Cf. I 172, 26 ff.   [53] Cf. Sermon XII, *passim*.   [54] Cf. I 177, 6 ff.

they shall be thrown into the depths of hell.[55]   And had not the Virgin Mary been humble, the Holy Ghost never would have come to her, regardless of other virtues she might have possessed.[56]   The latter declaration reminds the speaker to resume his denunciations against women—their vanity, and clothing.[57]

No matter how humble a person might be, he could never attain eternal happiness if he were hateful or envious,[58] and participated in the dance which divests one of humility.[59]

Berthold corrects, by the way, the misconception held by many of the worldly-minded that virtue implies the application of simple points of etiquette; [60] being polite, and knowing how to use a napkin does, as such, not mean that the person is virtuous.[61]

The preacher immediately asserts, furthermore, that heaven, as a goal, is praiseworthy, but the attainment of virtue is still better. He tells his listeners that the saints of God have indeed gained security through their eternal reward. However, while they are happy in their possession, they may no longer increase their measure of reward while we yet in the flesh can by our virtuous efforts, add daily to our portion.

Daz ist, sie habent vil mêr freude in himelrîche danne wir hie. An dém teile habent sie ez bezzer und an andern dingen, und daz sie himelrîche niht verliesen mugent. Daz mugen wír wol verliesen. Dar an hât ez sant Pêter bezzer und ander heiligen in himele. Sô haben wir ez an éinem teile bezzer danne sant Pêter und dan ander heiligen. Daz ist an guoten tugenthaften werken, daz wir alle tage, die wîle wir leben, sô mugen wir mit tugenden gar grôzen lôn verdienen. Swie vil sie freude hânt, sô haben wir ez doch bezzer an dém teile, wan swaz sant Pêter habe, daz habe im. Im wirt niht mêr. Er mac den hûfen niemer mêr groezer gemachen dan er hiute hât. . . . An dém teile haben wir ez bezzer, daz wir mit tugenden . . . den hûfen mêren mugen . . . von tage ze tage . . . sô mugen wir den hûfen ie groezer und groezer machen. . . . An dém teile ist tugent bezzer danne himelrîche.   (II 178, 13 ff.)

Mention has already been made that Berthold discourses only meagerly upon the virtues, in comparison to the somewhat lengthy

[55] Cf. I 476, 23 ff. Cf. also B. Schweizer, *Berthold von Regensburg—die vier Stricke des Teufels* (Diessen a. A.), Spalte 1. (Bruchstück . . . unbekannt. Wurde am 9. Dezember, 1922 aufgefunden.)

[56] Cf. I 53, 38 ff.   [59] Cf. I 173, 2.
[57] Cf. I 173, 3 f.   [60] Cf. II 179, 5 ff.; I 96, 24 ff.
[58] Cf. I 573, 28.   [61] Cf. I *ibid.*

treatments he accords the vices. Therefore, material on humility, as such, too, is scant. Berthold is not unique in this respect however. Hugo von Trimberg, Berthold's contemporary, also treats humility very lightly. Of Hugo, Götting says (p. 52): " Die Demut hat bei Hugo eigentümlicherweise keine eingehende Behandlung. Vielleicht, weil sie die spezifische Tugend des Mönchs ist." The latter statement agrees with, and shows influence of St. Benedict's view of humility. St. Benedict conceived humility as " une attitude d'âme habituelle qui règle l'ensemble des relations du moine avec Dieu dans la vérité de sa double qualité de créature pécheresse et d'enfant adoptif." [62] Berthold addressed himself, moreover,—in his sermon on the Seven Virtues—expressly to the lay people: " iu laien . . ."

In the case of Berthold's treatment of humility, it is safe to say that, because of his inadequate discussion, it is difficult to find leads which assist in throwing more light upon this question. Wolfram von Eschenbach had, not long before Berthold, delineated in the person of Parzival a man who ultimately acquired the virtue of humility. The Cluniac monks had preached humility in the previous century. Perhaps Berthold followed the example of his teacher David.

B. AVARICE

Avarice is frequently referred to throughout all the sermons of Berthold as the worst and most harmful evil which exists in the whole world; it is one of the capital sins which Berthold discusses at greatest length and with most vehemence. To Berthold the avaricious person is a combination of: *rouber, fürkoufer, wuocherer, dingesgeber; trügener an koufe, an hantwerke; symonîte, sacrilê-jer;* [63] *tiuvel; verköufer gotes zît.* [64]

One of Berthold's complaints against the avaricious, who are the most miserable of all sinners, is the disgraceful and iniquitous manner in which they waste their God-given time. [65] The preacher himself wonders how they will stand final judgment [66] because they never permit God to rest since,

---

[62] Cf. T. Tanquerey, *op. cit.*, 710. Cf. J. Elmendorf, *Elements of Moral Theology Based on the Summa Theologiae of St. Thomas Aquinas* (New York, 1892), 480; also Tanquerey, *op. cit.*, 711.
[63] Cf. II 69, 28 ff.; 183, 6 ff. [65] Cf. I 20, 11 ff.
[64] Cf. I 21, 13; 16. [66] Cf. *ibid.*, 9; II 30, 24; 32, 7 f.

3

Swie aber diu zît ist, sô geruowest dû, gîtiger, niemer. Dû gîtiger, gehabe dich wol! dû bist aber eines halben pfenninges rîcher worden sît ich iezuo von dir redende was. Dû sitzest verre unschedelîcher dînes guotes danne dise arme liute, wan die sûment sich iezuo unde gewinnent niht alse dû, wan dû gewinnest in der messe, in der predige, in der mettîn, an dem heiligen kristtage, an dem heiligen karfrîtage, an dem ôstertage. . . . Nû sich, gîtiger, wie dû got die zît widerreiten wellest! . . . nû sitzest dû verhertet und hâst aller wâren riuwe niht sô vil als einigen tropfen.

(I 21, 3 ff.)

To other sinners, who might have used valuable time in playing dice, dancing, or in unchastity, Berthold counsels true repentance for God's sake; but the avaricious would let the preacher labor in vain.[67] They are certain of being condemned to hell, because:

Dû bist in den zehen geboten in ir zwein, dû bist in den siben houbetsünden, dû bist der sünder einer, dem nieman keine gnâde tuot an der buoze. . . . Sô bist dû der sünder einer, vor dem got niemer ruowe gewinnet. Nû sich, gîtiger, wie maniger leie verdampnisse an dîner sünde lît! Sô bist dû ouch der sünder einer, des pîn unde marter sich von tage ze tage ze helle mêret unde wehset iemer mêre. Sô bist dû ouch der sünder einer, der sich niht alleine ze helle bringet, dû bringest ouch ander liute mit dir zer helle. Dû bist ouch der sünder einer, der dâ niuwe fünde vindet ûf die sünde. Dû bist ouch der sünder einer, der von unrehter vorhte unde von unrehter liebe verdampt wirt. . . .   (I 41, 17 ff.)

Berthold reminds those who accuse God of unequal distribution of goods, that the guilt lies on the vile method of the avaricious individual who steals and unjustly accumulates property; for God has created adequately to supply the needs of the people.[68] Avarice prompts one to hoard his ill-gotten goods; to let them rot rather than distribute them at the proper price.[69]

Poor people are cautioned to be constantly on guard against those who tend to avarice; and they should never expect to recover that which has been taken from them by souls hardened to justice.

Ir armen liute, ir freuwet iuch âne nôt, ir waenet allez, sie wellen iu gelten unde widergeben durch mîner predige willen, oder ir waenet des, sie wellen milte werden. . . . Jâ predigete got selbe einem gîtigen drithalb jâr unde half an im niht, unz daz er den prediger verkoufte umbe drîzic pfenninge.

(I 60, 7 ff. Cf. I 75, 2 ff.)

---

[67] Cf. I 21, 18 ff.   [68] Cf. I 59, 26 ff.

[69] Cf. *ibid.*, 39 f.; 258, 25 ff. Cf. also G. Schnürer, *Kirche und Kultur im Mittelalter* (Paderborn, 1929), Bd. II 423 f.

Those who serve the devil through avarice are imprecated since they cause thousands of other souls to be thrown into hell:

Owê, gîtiger, daz dich die wüetenden hunde ab dîner muoter brüste niht zarten unde daz dîner muoter ir brüste niht erdorreten, daz sô manic tûsent sêle von dînen schulden iht verlorn waeren!

(1 209, 13 ff. Cf. 258, 15 ff.)

Old people make the devil very happy because they seem more prone to avarice. They fear death; they can no longer participate in dancing, quarreling, unchastity, or go about with pride, hence they fall victim more easily to the devil's temptation, to avarice.[70] Children, too, are instructed to be careful to repudiate ill-gotten property inherited from their parents.[71] Even if the stolen goods are accepted after the donor's death, the heir will be condemned.[72] He admonishes young priests in particular to impose penance, accordingly, to all sinners but the avaricious—they must first make complete restitution.[73]

It does not suffice the covetous person to *murder* his own soul; he murders also the souls of his children and all who might fall heir to his unjust gains.[74] In this way he continues to murder even after his death, inasmuch as his heirs and their heirs will be lost.[75]

Berthold enumerates the points which both the devil and the avaricious have in common:

Daz êrste ist, daz der tiuvel staetes sündet tac unde naht für sich dar, daz er niemer geruowet keine wîle noch deheine stunde. Daz ander, daz er gîtic nâch den sünden ist: sô er ie mêr gesündet, sô er ie gerner sündet, und in benüeget eht niemer. Daz dritte ist, daz der tiuvel sich niemer bekêren wil. (I 243, 33 ff.)

Berthold says it has been pointed out by God himself that none is so calloused as the covetous; that even He could not convert an avaricious person unless He bought him over for thirty pfennigs.[76] The preacher warns other priests and confessors of what they shall have to contend with, and adds that he has never yet seen one

---

[70] Cf. I 486, 19 ff.; 417, 5 ff. Berthold says he can accomplish nothing with old people, " wan eht altiu gurre bedarf wol fuoters." (I 419, 22 ff.)
[71] Cf. I 193, 32 ff. [74] Cf. I 136, 7 ff.
[72] Cf. ibid., 16 ff. [75] Cf. ibid., 16 ff; II 149. 19 ff., 167, 27 f.
[73] Cf. I 195, 14 ff. [76] Cf. I 519, 17 ff.; 344, 11 ff.; II 52, 13.

culpable of avarice make full restitution.[77] Greed has turned him
into stone, and neither sermon nor confession, neither refined nor
coarse talks will help because he is even harder than the diamond
that cannot be broken by the heaviest blows of a hammer.[78]
Many think that if one preaches vociferously against avarice, it
is directed only to usurers, but,

Ez sint ouch die dâ lîhent ûf geltende guot, wan der tuot ez durch die
gîtikeit. Daz er zehen pfunt umb ein guot müeste geben daz im ze jâre
niwan ein pfunt widergulte, daz waere ouch mit gote unde mit rehte. . . .
Sô wirt ofte ein man noetic, er sî ritter oder kneht . . . der wirt sînes
eigen unde sînes lêhens ungerne ze durnehte âne unde denket in sînem
muote: ' ich wil daz guot versetzen: ez kumet noch der tac daz ich ez lîhte
loese oder mîner kinde einz.' Und er versetzet daz guot. Wolte er danne
rehte varn gegen gote der drûffe lîhet, der solte alsô drûf lîhen, daz er im
alliu jâr abe slüege waz daz guot gülte unz daz ez sich erlôste. (1 437, 26 ff.)
Swer joch anders lîhet und anders pfantschaft hât, dâ solte der jenem
gelten unde widergeben swaz ez im mêre vergiltet wan als er jenem drûf
gelîhen hât, alse verre und erz geleisten mac, unz an den hindersten pfen-
ninc, oder sîner verdampten sêle . . . muoz . . . in der helle brinnen.
(1 438, 9 ff.)

Others are guilty of avarice with preëmption.[79] For instance when
one says:

. . . ' ich gibe iu . . . vil wînes oder kornes . . . mir ist der pfenninge nôt,
die gebet mir iezuo her, sô gibe iu den kouf deste nâher als ich ez iu ge-
winne über vier wochen . . . oder ein halbez jâr.'   (1 438, 17 ff.)

Berthold informs the people that to the avaricious this seems
commendable usury—just as when the most wicked Jew lends a
shilling, and asks thirteen in return. There is unity of thought
and action between the covetous and heretics, and those who sin
against the Holy Ghost.[80] They form one company with Judas as
the manager, under whose banner and shield they associate.[81]

Berthold likens the covetous to grasshoppers: they have a coat of
armor, human-like countenances, women's heir, lion's teeth, and a
scorpion's tail.[82]

---

[77] Cf. I 519, 11 ff.
[78] Cf. I 418, 35 ff.; II 143, 36 ff.   [80] Cf. I 245, 17 ff.
[79] Cf. I 438, 16 f.   [81] Cf. *ibid.*, 262, 3 ff.; II 209, 7 ff.
[82] Cf. I 417, 24 ff.; II, 144, 17 ff. In another instance (I 555, 12), Berthold compares the avaricious with locusts.

Die heuschreken heten menschen-antlütze; daz bezeichent, daz dû ein
kristenmensche bist mit dem namen und ein jüde mit den werken . . .
lewenzene; daz bediutet, daz der lewe gar vil frezzen mac, unde dâ von
bezeichent daz den gîtigen, daz den nieman ersetten mac. Swie vil ein
gîtiger hât unde swie lützel ein armer man hât . . . der gîtige brichet
dannoch dem armen abe sîn armuot, swâ er kan unde mac, unde mêret
sînen grôzen rîchtuom dâ mite. . . . Sie heten ouch scorpenzegele. . . .
Der stichet gar übel des scorpen zagel. Daz bediutet, daz er alle die werlt
durchstichet mit sînen unrehten gewinnen. . . . Sie heten îsenîne halsberge
. . . daz bezeichent ir groesten unsaelde, daz sie sô veste sint an der gîtikeit
. . . sie sint sô gar versteinet . . . daz weder predige niht hilfet noch bîhte
. .. . noch süeziu rede. . . .   (I 418, 6 ff.)

Berthold almost despairs that his preachings to the avaricious are
in vain, yet they never permit him to rest:

Die von Samariâ unde die von Gomorrâ unde die von Sodomâ die lânt
mich geruowen . . . dû laest mich niemer geruowen, wan dîn pfluoc ist
eht alle zît . . . ûf der arbeit des gewinnes.   (I 244, 27 ff.)

Fasting on Saturdays and the six weeks before Christmas, found-
ing hospitals, making pilgrimages, or entering cloisters will not
help the covetous unless he goes to confession, amends his life, and
repays to the last farthing.[83] He must make a two-fold confession:
first to God, secondly to his fellowman.[84]

Finally, to those who would gain additional property by moving
the land-marker, Berthold says:

Pfî, welch ein geschrei über dich gât, gîtiger, an dem jungesten tage, sô
allez daz über dich schrîet dem dû ie keinen schaden getaete. Und sô man
dich verfluochet, sô sprichet . . . allez daz volk ' âmen '.   (II 217, 7 ff.)
Pfî dich, gîtiger, wie erklinget dîn âmen vor gotes ôren alse des hundes
bellen!   (I 109, 34 f.)

Avarice is thus one of Berthold's special objects of attack. From
the foregoing treatment, and additional discussion later in the
study, Berthold's sincere, meticulous, and sharp sense of justice
comes to the fore.

Theology defines avarice as being *the inordinate love of earthly
goods.* The greviousness of the vice lies in the fact that it destroys
the end for which God has given man earthly goods: for our own
benefit, and that of our neighbor. They were given to assist our

---

[83] Cf. II 48-49 *passim*; 123, 1 ff.   [84] Cf. II 41, 28 ff.

temporal necessities, to preserve our life and the life of our depend-
ents. Hence, avarice destroys the order in love of temporal matters.
The disorder lies in the intention, because persons might desire
wealth for its own sake, as an end in itself, or for other aims, for
example, to seek pleasures and honors. Furthermore, the manner
of seeking riches may be pursued regardless of the rights of others,
and to many other detriments. Avarice tends to make wealth in
possessions the supreme goal of one's life; he idolizes money, and
hoards it.

Berthold's further justification for exhorting the old as being
great offenders in this category of avarice, aside from their fear
that they can no longer participate in unchastity, etc., may be, as
he says, that youth is not prone to avarice because they are yet
improvident. But it is rather at an age when senility is approaching
that this sin comes into prevalence, for it is often then that the fear
of want develops. Here, then, Berthold might have mentioned that
bachelors and spinsters are not rarely exposed to avarice because
they have no offspring to care for them in old age.

Berthold's comparison of avaricious persons to grasshoppers is one
instance of the genuine *Volksprediger*: simple, illustrative language,
rich in meaning. If avarice is permitted to remain in one's heart,
he becomes hardened by the passion, mistrusts God, and exchanges
wealth for God. Hence, he also sins against charity by omitting
necessary love of neighbor and almsgiving.

b. *Virtue Opposed to Avarice: Almsgiving*

Man, according to Berthold, possesses freedom of will, allowing
him to choose between virtue and sin. But, Berthold continues,
Lucifer had this gift of free will, and he chose to do evil, and therefore was driven out of heaven; and angels, too, who made the
wrong choice were cast into the lowest depths of hell.[85] Therefore,
he who wants to avoid hell should do good, should especially strive
to acquire the virtue of charity—one of the noblest virtues—which
leads man to assist his fellow-Christian, and thus strive to imitate
Our Blessed Mother, and the thousands of saints who attained

---

[85] Cf. I 97, 13 ff. Wherever Berthold treats freedom of the will, it is in
accordance with the Dominican Theology of St. Thomas. Cf. Keil, *op. cit.*,
16.

heaven through charity.[86] Otherwise he may never be permitted
to enter the Kingdom of Heaven.[87] These are natural exaggera-
tions of a well-meaning, zealous monk who speaks to uneducated
masses, and eagerly encourages people to be generous to the Church
as well as to all poor people.

Charity is also one of the world's greatest virtues because it
makes one merciful toward the poor and needy,[88] and charity is
immeasurably useful to combat the snares of the devil.[89] As
opposed to covetousness, charity manifests itself chiefly in the form
of almsgiving. The rich are urged to be generous to those not so
blessed as themselves in worldly goods: they should give alms,
have Masses said, build roads, endow monasteries and hospitals,
feed the hungry, give drink to the thirsty, clothe the naked, and
give shelter.[90] Almsgiving in God's name obliterates sin and
increases the soul's happiness.[91]

To the covetous rich who do not practice charity, and to misers
who hoard the things merely lent them by God instead of helping
the poor, the preacher says:

Pfî, hördeler, wie tiure dir diu tugent ist . . . miltekeit! Des wirdest
dû ouch begraben an den grunt der helle, sam der rîche man. (I 60, 1 f.)
Dû hilfest in (the poor), daz sie vollen ze almuosenaeren werden müezen.
(I 58, 12 f.)

And to those who disregard the words of St. John, " gip den hungerigen z'ezzen," and who allow food to rot instead of selling it
cheaply:

Pfî, gîtiger! . . . daz dich die wolve in der wiegen niht gâzen, ê daz diu
werlt sô manigen gebresten von dir haete! (I 258, 15 ff.)

Finally, Berthold instructs both rich and poor to execute their good
intentions with good works, and be generous with lending in the
name of charity.[92]

[86] Cf. I 57, 35 ff. For the treatment accorded charity by the thirteenth
century didactic writers, cf. M. P. Goetz, *op. cit.*, 91-93, and footnotes;
cf. also C. T. Rapp, *op. cit.*, 56-63.
[87] Cf. I 177, 9.   [88] Cf. I 108, 28 f.   [89] Cf. I 476, 36 f.
[90] Cf. I 190, 12 ff.; 25, 30 ff. According to J. Bühler, *Die Kultur des
Mittelalters* (Leipzig, 1931), 316, homes for the aged and hospitals were
richly endowed.
[91] Cf. I 476, 38 ff.   [92] Cf. I 477, 14 ff.

Berthold's statement to the effect that almsgiving " obliterates " sin lacks clearness and tends to mislead because Berthold does not distinguish between venial and mortal sin in this instance. Only perfect contrition, of course, operates a forgiveness of sin, but, in case of mortal sin one must have the intention of going to confession within reasonable time. Venial sin can be forgiven apart from the Sacrament of Penance through other means. According to the secular creed, every material deed wrought to benefit a needy fellow-man is almsgiving. According to the creed of Christianity, however, almsgiving implies a spiritual as well as corporal service rendered to the poor for Christ's sake.[93] They differ in this that when operated through supernatural motives, the almsgiving is raised to a supernatural plane.

C. LUST

Among the multifarious temptations placed in the world by the devil, he reserved one especially for the young because he recognized its strong allure.[94] Lust serves the devil well to ensnare the souls of youth: they become easily addicted to it, and they feel more inclined toward it than to other sins.[95] But youth, as yet unstained by grave sins, as yet soft of heart, incorrupt, simple, may be more readily guided toward fasting and prayer and may be more amenable to teaching and instruction.[96] The devil seems to have less power over youth because by their inexperience they are more guileless; hence, sins such as avarice, gluttony, and pride are more or less foreign to them; they do yield, however, more readily to the sins of the flesh because the heart of man is inclined to this weakness from his youth.[97]

[93] Cf. *Catholic Encyclopedia*, I 328.

[94] Cf. I 411, 20 ff. ʿ'?, 3.

[95] Cf. I 411, 27 f., ɪᴏᴜ, 27. " Wan daz allez êrste ûz der schaln sliufet, daz bewillet sich nû mit der selben sünde: die dierne unde die knehte, die süne unde die töhter sint alles nescher unde nescherin, und ist halt als gewonlich diu selbe sünde und als gemeine worden, daz ir nû nieman ahtet und niht danne ein gespötte ist. Sô man in dâ von prediget, sô winket einer ûf den andern unde grüllet ûf in . . . unde trîbent alsô ir gespötte. . . . "

(I 82, 18 ff.)

[96] Cf. I 411, 29 ff., 480, 27 ff.; II 139, 10.

[97] Cf. I 411, 33 ff.

Regarding fornication, Berthold wishes to destroy the notion held by many that it is not so terrible and so great a sin as the priests make it out to be. He warns the congregation that if two unmarried persons committed this sin, and died thereafter without having repented, they must go straight to hell, and the prayers of all the priests, monks, nuns, saints and angels in behalf of the transgressors would be of no avail.[98] One who persists in committing unlawful sexual intercourse is vitriolically rebuked by Berthold:

... dû wellest mit der unê umbe gên, sô nim niuwer eine zer unê : sô nim die selbe an éine hant unde den tiuvel an die ándern hant unde gêt alle driu mit einander hin zer helle. . . . (I 279, 4 ff.)

Those who perform unchaste actions with consecrated persons are commanded to choose between severe atonement for their sins, or to suffer eternally in hell:

Pfî, dû schantflecke . . . die dâ bî gewîhten liuten ligent unde sich lâzent tasten mit den henden, dâ mite man der meide sun handelt! Vil wunderlîchen balde in starke buoze oder an den grunt der hellen! (1 452, 22 ff. Cf. 205, 30 ff.)

And to those who sin with nuns, or monks who have taken their vows in the cloisters,

... die sint sâ zehant in dem hoehsten banne, ez sîn frouwen oder man. Ob man sie niemer ze banne getuot, sô sint sie doch in dem hoehsten banne, den got in himel oder ûf erden hât. . . . (I 452, 27 ff. Cf. II 69, 10 ff.)

To this, Berthold adds ne would rather die without reception of Holy Communion than assist at Mass in the same Church with such a person;[99] and he would rather not hear Mass, did he know that the celebrant ever committed an unchaste act with a woman.[100]

The unmarried are frequently told to heed the advice of St. Paul: "fliehet die unkiusche," because this vice deprives them not only of health and long-life, but it also damns their souls.[101]

Diu selbe sünde ie seltener getân ie bezzer an lîbe und an sêle unde an der gnâde gotes. . . . Wellet ir des niht tuon, vil wunderlîchen balde von der gesuntheit des lîbes unde von lanclebenne iuwers lîbes . . . in den lôn

---

[98] Cf. I 568, 15 ff.　　　　[99] Cf. I 452, 30 ff.
[100] Cf. II 69, 12 ff.; I 130, 17. Berthold would remain from Mass for ten years (I 206, 15).
[101] Cf. I 483, 2 ff., 178, 12.

nâch den sünden zuo dem êwigen tôde, nû des êrsten an der sêle und an
dem jungesten tage an lîbe und an sêle!

. . . .

Sô wirt der blint, sô wirt der lam; dû maht halt ûzsetzic werden von
unmâze der stinkenden sünde, diu toetelt. Selbe taete, selbe habe. Daz
dû dir selber gebriuwen habest, daz trink ouch selber. (1 435, 8 ff.; 19 ff.)

In addition, the unmarried who perform unchaste deeds might
have to bear the disgrace of begetting illegitimate children who
will never be able to attain either ecclesiastical or secular positions
of honor.[102] Berthold suggests repeatedly that the young marry,
and not live like cattle, lest they lose their souls through harlotry.[103]

. . . ir jungen liute, vil wunderlîchen balde ze der heiligen ê, . . . Und
alse dû man oder dû frouwe niuwen ze éinem mâle zer unê mit einander sît,
sô habet ir eine houbetsünde getan unde wirt iuwer beider niemer rât. . . .
Dâ tuont dise liute in der heiligen ê drîzic jâr . . . sehzic, alse lange sô
sie lebent, rehte daz selbe daz ouch dû tuost, unde die gevarnt niemer zer
helle drumbe, sie enirre danne ander sünde.   (I 307, 19 ff.)

With regard to lust, Berthold also flays poor people as being
addicted to it, and the part they play in furthering this vice is
sinful:

Die armen liute. . . . Daz sint die dâ unfuore trîbent, die umb ein genä-
schelîn zwei in eine kamer stôzent. Sich, alliu diu werlt diu möhte dîne
martel niht erlîden, die dû dar umbe lîden muost. Dû bist gar vinnic an
der sêle.   (I 121, 31 ff.)

Bawds and procurers who drive out God's grace from many a pure
soul, and who can join more people in two or four weeks than the
devil can in ten years, will receive their reward in hell with Judas.[104]

---

[102] Cf. I 178, 17 ff. "Sie sülnt ze rehte niemer prêlaten werden in
deheinen konvente noch werltlîche . . . noch geistlîche rihter noch pfarrer.
. . . Dû muost ein basthart sîn êlôs und erbelôs" (I 413, 26 ff.). Cf. also
Keil, *op. cit.*, 118.

[103] Cf. I 278, 26 ff.; II 92, 34 ff.; 140, 31 ff. The preacher elaborates upon
this, addressing a young man: ". . . nim ûz aller der werlte eine zer ê, dâ
dû rehte . . . mite lebest . . . Wellest dû einer kurzen niht, sô nim eine
lange; . . . unde wiltû einer wîzen niht, sô nim eine swarze . . . nim . . .
eine êlîche frouwe"   (I 278, 30 ff.)

[104] Cf. I 208, 6 ff., 335, 31. Speaking to the people, Berthold says: ". . .
ir soltet sie ûz der stat slahen, wan ir habet êrbaere hûsfrouwen. Unde tuot
ir des niht, sô müget ir wol leidigen schric dâ von geleben" (I 208, 11 ff.,
335, 36 ff.).

They shall all be damned because they murder thousands of souls, take money for their evil deeds,[105] teach children to go astray,[106] and because they are *des tiuvels jagehunt*,[107] *des tiuvels blâsbalc*,[108] and *des tiuvels fürmunt*.[109] Berthold regrets that women of illrepute should have ever been baptized:

Pfî, daz ie dehein touf ûf dich kam! (1 336, 5 f.)

Because " Man seit mir ein ungelouplîchez maere, daz ein diernelîn mit einem sî hin wec geloufen, daz ist niuwer aht jâr alt," Berthold commands parents to keep strict vigilance over their children, even in Church.[110] After Mass, they should be particularly attentive that their sons and daughters are not approached and tricked by the waiting procurers.[111] Lack of proper supervision over children may be the cause of their downfall: [112] these children take advantage of their freedom; like mice and worms they sneak from one corner to another.[113] They fall into bad company, and from the resultant evil familiarity, often commit unchaste acts.[114] Berthold delineates vices common among young persons which must be avoided since they induce lust:

. . . boese geluste des fleisches, sô dem menschen zem êrsten wol ist in sînem gemüete mit dem geluste der unkiusche . . . der gerne schentlîche rede dâ von rett, und der ez gerne hoeret reden. Daz dritte schentlich gesiht, mit den ougen schelklichen hin und her fliegen. Daz vierde daz schentlich küssen. Daz fünfte diu schentlich begrîfunge der lider. Daz sehste . . . diu schentlîchen werc und unkiusche selbiu. (II 140, 20 ff.)

Adolescents are urged to protect the purity with which they enter this world, but, should they find it difficult to bear the *wîzen wât,* Berthold says they must heed the advice of St. Paul and enter matrimony.[115]

Besides the contributory vices which lust engenders,[116] Berthold offers supplementary reasons to dissuade the guilty. Still on the subject of unchastity, he says:

---

[105] Cf. II 219, 33; 38.
[106] Cf. II 189, 18.
[107] II 219, 35.
[108] I 319, 18.
[109] I 336, 8.
[110] Cf. I 470, 2 ff.
[111] Cf. *ibid.*, 5 ff.
[112] Cf. I 469, 39 f.
[113] Cf. I 483, 13 ff.
[114] Cf. I 470, 11 ff.
[115] Cf. I 412, 8 ff.
[116] They are stealing, dancing, murder, hatred, envy, enmity, pride (I 192, 22 ff.), inordinate love of body (I 177, 12.), and gluttony (I 177, 18 f.).

. . . smecket sie als ein fûlez âs? Nein, sie niht! . . . als ein fûler kaese? Nein . . . als ein fûler visch? Nein . . . als ein fûler mist? ' Nein, sie niht! Ich sage dir . . . weder minner noch mê, wan dû rehte toetelst. Daz bediutet ze glîcher wîse, daz dû dem tôde iesâ naeher bist.

(I 178, 25 ff. Cf. 434, 30 ff.)

Berthold makes several statements that would allude to the rampancy, in his times, of unlawful sexual intercourse. By many it was then not regarded as a serious sin; this more or less licenses those who entertain such an attitude to indulge freely in venereal pleasures. Bawds and procurers made advances even after Mass; furthermore, they must have often met with success if " they could join more people, in sin, in two or four weeks than the devil would in ten years."

For a priest, even six hundred years ago, to mention to his congregation that he would not assist at Mass and would deny himself the Viaticum if the minister thereof had sinned with women, is unquestionably a severe pronouncement. Berthold, frequently prone to exaggeration, undoubtedly wished in this instance to emphasize the malice of this sin, and to instill fear into his hearers against its commission.

Berthold preaches, moreover, of occasions leading to lust which even to-day are the axioms of preachers and spiritual writers. They warn against the occasions that persons encounter, whether in themselves or in their surroundings which can be overcome only by mortification: touch, kissing, sight, familiarity, speech, and lewd songs.[117]

c. *Virtue Opposed to Lust: Chastity*

Lust which has become so common that many regard it to be of no consequence and shame, must be combatted with chastity, (*kiusche*), one of the noblest virtues known to the world.[118] The preacher frequently cites the Blessed Virgin as the model of chastity because one sings, and reads about her, that she never glanced at

---

[117] Cf. St. Thomas Aquinas, IIa IIae q. 64 a. 4; cf. Tanquerey, *op. cit.*, II 559 f.

[118] Cf. I 105, 29 ff. The sense of shame being indeed valuable as a protection against unchastity, is discussed by J. Mausbach, *Die katholische Moral und Ihre Gegner* (Köln, 1913), 103-105.

man with desire and coyness, and that the heart of no man ever bore a sensual thought against her.[119] Berthold extends high praise to persons who have preserved the chastity with which they were born, and have the intention of keeping it until they die.[120] Young people are urged to meditate on God; to pray fervently to the Virgin Mary that she protect their chastity through the purity with which she was overshadowed by the Holy Ghost.[121] Furthermore, they should pray that, through the goodness of the Blessed Virgin and her holy Son, they be protected as were St. Catherine, St. Agatha, the good St. Nicholas, St. Ulrich, and thousands of other saints.[122] Chastity is preserved above all through personal modesty, chaste thoughts and actions; one must avoid bad companions and evil intimacy.[123] Another means to chastity is the evasion of flighty thoughts, boasting, immoderate laughter, the exchange of lustful, craving glances at parties or dances; and modesty in clothing, word, and manner.[124] Berthold stresses the importance of chaste thoughts and explains his point by example: when a man (or woman) goes into a shop to look around, has no intention of making a purchase, and fixes his gaze upon a handsome, or well-dressed individual, yet has no thought of committing sin—that is merely legitimate amusement. If he entered there merely for pastime, and not to buy—if he bargains for clothes regardless—and converses with a beautiful woman close by, yet if the thought of sinning with her does not enter his mind, it is still not a mortal sin. However, when he stands in front of the shop so long that he craves to make a purchase, and then bargains at such length and indicates that he heartily desires the article, and nothing but lack of money restrains him—then he acts in accordance with the ways of the devil. The same applies to thoughts.[125]

Unchastity is so enticing that scarcely anyone may escape it; chastity, on the other hand, is so meritorious that the virgins in heaven are rewarded with special crowns.[126] Therefore parents

---

[119] Cf. I 256, 3 ff.   [121] Cf. I 481, 12 ff.   [123] Cf. *ibid.*, 21 ff.
[120] Cf. I 105, 36 ff.   [122] Cf. *ibid.*, 17 ff.   [124] Cf. *ibid.*, 25 ff.
[125] Cf. I 482, 6 ff.   Cf. also G. Frassinetti, *Compendio della Teologia Morale di S. Alfonso* (Genoa, 1866), I 118.
[126] Cf. I 526, 2 ff.

28   *The German Sermons of Berthold von Regensburg*

must instruct, and seek to confirm their children in the ways of chastity while they are still at a tender age. Parents must not be amused when children imitate the improper actions of men and women.[127] Berthold says married people, too, should resist unchastity:

Ir liute, ir müget ouch der unkiusche widerstên. Iuwer leben heizet niht unkiusche in der heiligen ê, swenne ir iuwer zuht behaltet und iuwer mâze.

(I 106, 1 ff.)

He instructs them how to be virtuous by exercising self-control which is fitting and proper not only in church, on the street, and at table, but also in their marital relations.[128] This is what God desires of married people, for many souls have been lost through *unzuht* and *unmâze*.[129] The moralist elaborates upon this by naming the five times in the year when married couples are to refrain from what he calls *unkiuschen dingen* because

. . . ir habet dannoch zîte rehte genuoc: ein langez jâr habet ir manige zît iuwer geslehte ze mêren, daz ir kinde gar genuoc gewinnet.

(I, 322, 8 ff.)

And besides,

Ez ist halt vil krêatûre, diu niwan éin zît in dem jâre hât; sô hat iu got gar vil zît gelân in dem langen jâre, unde dâ von ist daz gar mügelich, daz ir die fünf zît mâze haltet unde maezclîchen sît mit einander an dem bette.

(I 322, 11 ff.)

Then the medievalist announces the "holy, forbidden times:"[130]

[127] Cf. I 483, 17 ff., 256, 15 ff.
[128] Cf. I 321, 39 ff. For information on chastity among earlier peoples, and the views of St. Paul and St. Augustine, cf. F. Cabrol, *Dictionnaire D'Archéologie Chrétienne et De Liturgie* (Paris, 1913), T. Troisième, première partie, 1145 ff.
[129] Cf. I 322, 2 ff. ". . . triuwe hoeret zuo dem bette. Wan ez vellet manic tûsent sêle von dem bette in die helle, daz ir niemer mêre rât wirt, halt ûz der heiligen ê. Swie heilic diu ê sî, dû maht dînem gemechede als ungetriuwe sîn ze dem bette an sîner sêle, daz iuwer deweders niemer rât wirt" (1 321, 28 ff.).
[130] The following material and citations appearing without footnote references are found in I 322-328 *passim*. For allied material, cf. II, Sermon LV, *passim*. Cf. also Keil, *op. cit.*, 106 f. In another instance, consideration is even given to the time any sin is committed: "Ez ist gar sünde der eine sünde an dem mântage tuot. Tuot er sie aber an dem

Daz êrste zît ist, wenne man gemeinlîchen vastet, in der goltvasten unde
die vierzic tage vor ôstern. Diu ander zît ist, als man gemeinlîchen diu
kriuze treit an sant Markes tage, unde die drîe tage vor pfingesten. Unde
diu dritte ist, sô die frouwen in kindelbette ligent.

Berthold interrupts the continuation of the sermon to enlarge upon
the third period. For six weeks after childbirth, men ought to
refrain from carnal intercourse; they ought to be kind and patient
with their wives, for they have suffered long enough. Women, too,
receive instruction: during the stated times, they should hold their
husbands off, and never permit them to remain too long in their
presence. They should not tolerate husbands in too close proximity,
for this might excite the passions.

Diu vierde zît ist ein zît, dâ der almehtige got gar griulîchen von redet.
Daz ist, sô die frouwen kranc sint; sô sult ir des gar wol gehüeten . . .
waeret ir halt zwei jâr von in gewesen, ir soltet ez wol gehüeten daz ir sîn
in dér zît iemer keinen muot gewünnet.

Women must inform their husbands of these times. Men must
not seek an explanation when their wives tell them " to lie down
and dream; " that " they have headaches; " and men must not even
touch their wives during this period. Married couples should imitate the Jewish custom in these times, in order to safeguard themselves against uniting.[131]

Diu fünfte zît ist, swelhes tages man gebiutet ze vîgern, die selben naht sô
man des morgens vîgern sol, des nahtes sol man sich kiusche halten unde
des morgens allen den selben tac den man vîgert unz hin ze naht.

Here Berthold declares that he is certain that women will follow
and understand his thoughts more than men. Men desire freedom

suntage, sô ist sie aber sünder. Sô diu zît ie hoeher unde heiliger ist, sô diu
sünde ie groezer unde swaerer ist, die man dran begêt " (I 128, 28 ff.).
[131] " . . . seht wol, daz ein stinkender jüde, der uns an böcket, der
schônet der selben zît gar wol unde halt mit gar grôzem flîze. Wan als diu
jüdinne einen knopf gestricket an ein lînlachen unde henket daz an ir bette:
alle die wîle unde der jüde den knopf dâ siht hangen, alle die wîle sô fliuhet
der jüde daz bette als den tiuvel. Unde dâ von sult ir der selben zît gar
wol schônen unde hüeten " (I 323, 12 ff.). Elsewhere (I 309, 18 ff.).
Berthold says: " Juden . . . daz sîn êliute, witwen, oder meide, die sint
alle vorteiles verdampt." For further information on Jewish marital
customs, cf. *The Jewish Encyclopedia* (New York and London, 1904), VIII,
336 ff.

in all things, *unde koment dâ mite in die frîheit, daz sie keiner zît wellent schônen*. Because *wir vinden ofte, daz die frouwen kiuscher sint danne die man,* women must always do the best they can to make their husbands behave. However, if a man becomes brutal and persistent, and the wife is forced to submit, then, whether it be holy Christmas Eve, or the Eve of Good Friday, *sô tuo ez mit trûrigem herzen; wan sô bist dû unschuldic, ist eht dîn wille dâ bî niht.* But, *ie seltsaener ie bezzer . . . dâ von sult ir die mâze halten . . . in der ê mit der kiusche.*

It seems that Berthold cannot sufficiently stress the importance of chastity in marriage. With regard to the stated " five times," he asserts that God Himself commanded the same in the " Book of Chastity," which mankind ought to record in gold. *All* children conceived during these " times " will never add joy to parents, because they will be either affected by the devil, leprous, epileptic, hunchbacked, blind, deformed, mute, weak-minded, or they may be born with multifarious physical deformities. Then it will be too late to repair the damage. " *Selbe tuo, selbe habe. Daz dû dir selber habest gebriuwen, daz trink ouch selber ûz.*" Berthold becomes even more definite and declares that if what he says does not happen, the children shall surely die an undeserving death. What has been stated happens, however, for the most part to *geuliuten* and *unverstendigen liuten.* To noblemen and townsmen it does not happen, for they are prudent people; they frequently listen to sermons, assist at Mass, and know when husbands and wives should remain apart from each other. Country people, on the other hand, seldom listen to sermons, and work late into the night. They sleep like stones and look after nothing. On a holiday when they remain at home and should rest, their wives clad themselves scantily, and the men rush *als ein hane,* and both disregard the time and the hour. Such is not chastity, and should a child be conceived, the parents will never experience joy with this child. Berthold says further that married people pay God greater honor by observing chastity.

Still another means for preserving chastity in marriage is *zuht an dem bette gar mit flîze.* Unfortunately, Berthold says, he dare not expatiate at length on this topic however necessary it might be ; he dare not speak in the presence of perverts and mockers—for already they are contemplating to pervert that about which he is speaking; they have evil tongues. Nevertheless, he changes his mind: *Iedoch sage ich iu ein wênic . . . ein vil wunder wênic, daz ir niht gar âne zuht an dem bette sît.* Since the time of Adam and Eve, God intended the wife to be subject to the husband. But now, women have become so bold they quarrel as if possessed by the devil—they scarcely enter the room unless they start a battle. *Man suln strîten unde frouwen suln spinnen.* Berthold is conscious of his intentional vagueness:

' Bruder Berhtolt, ich enweiz niht, was dû meinest.' Sich, daz ist mir daz aller liebeste; got helfe mir, daz dû mich niht verstêst. Aber ein schalkhaft herze verstêt mich wol.

Berthold laments that he must be so plain for the good of some people, and continues:

Ich meine als frouwen mannes gewant an legent. Der dâ verstê, der verstê. Ein man sol ein man sîn, ein frouwe sol ein frouwe sîn. Unde dannoch für baz ander unzuht. Der almehtige got hât alliu dinc geschaffen an ir stat. . . . Ein schalkhaft herze verstê mich wol.

He repeats that he is glad if some among them are yet so guileless that they do not fully comprehend him.

To the inquiry whether man may do with his wife whatever he pleases, Berthold replies emphatically in the negative, and adds:

Dîn mezzer ist ouch dîn eigen mezzer: dâ mite soltû doch ir die kelen niht abe snîden.

Then he reminds his auditors that if they do not observe *zuht unde mâze,* they shall be condemned; *zuht unde mâze überhabent iuch der helle.* Ignorance is not condoned.

Berthold beseeches those who are still virgins to remain so until their death—that they may stand honorably and uprightly on the day of final judgment. Virgins receive the greatest reward in heaven.[132]

He also counsels the three types of widows [133] in ways of chastity

[132] Cf. 11 193, 24. Luther regards virginity as an impossible state; cf. C. Poulet, *Church History,* Trans. by Raemers (St. Louis and London, 1935), Vol. 11, 28.

[133] " Welt ir nû wizzen, wâ von ir witewen heizet? Seht daz ist darumbe. Iu ist wîte wê allenthalben, daz ist iuwer name: wîte wê! wîte wê! "
(II 193, 20 ff.)

so that they may endear themselves to God. Those "widows" who lost their virginity outside of marriage, and have repented and have made a firm purpose of amendment, are close to God; [134] but those who surrendered their virginity by marriage, and lead chaste lives after their husband's death, are dearer to God.[135] Nevertheless, God prefers above all, those "widows" who willingly separate from their husbands to enter a cloister. But Berthold discourages this: "Des wil ich rehte aber niht, daz ez darumbe ieman tuo," because "ez ist manic alter schedel, mir gaebe in sîn hûsfrouwe umbe driu eier ûf . . ." [136]

Berthold's references to "forbidden times" in his treatment of chastity call to mind the fact that present day theologians agree that there exists in positive law no prohibition of time with regard to the enjoyment of the privileges of marriage.[137] It is true that some of the early penitential books contained prohibitions no longer countenanced in the Church, but these books, although widely in vogue, were not always authentic nor had they always the force of law. Cicognani says, "Into these books (Poenitentialia) enormous in number, crept abuses and penances arbitrarily imposed." [138] Some of these books were even condemned by councils.[139] Berthold's preaching and teaching was undoubtedly influenced by some of these "Libri Poenitentiales," perhaps the *Poenitentiale Ecclesiarum Germaniae* which forbids the very acts against which Berthold inveighs.[140]

The "Book of Chastity" to which Berthold refers must be a figurative term. Research in theological writings makes no mention thereof.

The rational motive of the virtue of chastity is the reasonableness of controlling sexual appetite in the married and excluding it in the unmarried, as also of seeking and expressing it in marriage in a rational way, unless the exercise of some higher virtue or more pressing duty justify complete continence, temporary or perpetual,

---

[134] Cf. II 192, 9 ff.; I 186, 39 ff.

[135] Cf. II 192, 25 ff.   [136] Cf. *ibid.*, 27 ff.

[137] Cf. H. Noldin, *Theologia Moralis,* I 85, sec. 81. Etc.

[138] A. Cicognani, *Canon Law* (Philadelphia, 1938), 229.

[139] A. Van Hove, *Prolegomena,* 119, sec. 135.

[140] Cf. J. Mueller, "Abusus Matrimonii," in *Theologisch-praktische Quartalschrift,* 1922, No. 1, 111-112.

without prejudice to the rights of others. Chastity is a virtue for
every state of life. This virtue connotes a great victory over an
imperious appetite. Few persons of adult age are immune from
the incitement and allurement of this appetite. The practice of
the virtue is usually arduous, is highly meritorious, gives man a
great mastery over himself in this respect, and is pleasing to God.[141]

D. GLUTTONY

Berthold frequently associates gluttony with unchastity, and
attributes the former to an inordinate love of the body which
causes thousands of souls to be damned. In one instance he bitterly
reproves Solomon, who, he says, despite his wisdom, was a fool;
for he had more than inordinate love of body—he had sixty queens,
eighty duchesses and countesses who were his concubines.[142] Every
day their meals consisted of thirty oxen, exclusive of the fish and
game.[143] Berthold appropriately comments:

Pfî, trenker unde frâz! daz ist dîner frâzheit unde wollust ungelîch, wan
disiu untugent heizet unkiusche des lîbes unde des mundes unde wollust des
lîbes.   (I 177, 18 ff.)

And then he turns upon Solomon:

Unde hâst dû ez niht gebüezet, Salomôn, dû muost als lange in der helle
sîn alse got ein herre in dem himel ist.   (I 177, 28 ff.)

The preacher says that the unchaste, and those who do not fast
out of love for God, and those who are still chaste but tend to
indolence, should flock together like birds of a feather.[144] And to
the inquiry, "Ist iendert dehein frâz hie?" Berthold declares he
is afraid there is a great number in the audience who shall have to
forfeit eternal bliss through gluttony.[145] Such people reserve themselves for the devil by their inordinate love for these two vices
(gluttony and unchastity) which are stimuli for falling even into
greater sins.[146]

It is no wonder that the gluttonous shall be condemned—like
Esau, they sit and eat to such excess that their stomachs expand

[141] H. Davis, S. J., *Moral and Pastoral Theology* (London, 1938), II 173.
[142] Cf. I 177, 20 ff.
[143] Cf. *ibid.*, 17 f.
[144] Cf. I 367, 10 ff.
[145] Cf. *ibid.*
[146] Cf. I 40-41 *passim.*

four times their normal size.[147] Berthold entreats the guilty to abandon their evil practices which deprive them of health and long life.[148] Gluttony is so injurious to the body, that no one can fully describe the resultant evil effects. However, Berthold says he must impart some information, " *als vil ich dâ weiz,*" so as to assist many in curbing the habit which does them great harm. In many of his sermons where reference is made to this vice, the preacher ordinarily states that he directs no statements to the poor, because " *ir habet mit dér sünde niht ze schaffen, wan ir habet selten die nôtdurft;* " and because " *wan daz ir ze rehter nôt haben soltet, daz bringent dise fraeze für mit übermâze.*"

Berthold is conscious of the false impression maintained by some that frequent partaking of food assures one of greater strength, and hence, longer life. He corrects the misapprehension by an anatomical explanation. The stomach, which lies directly in the center of the body, is first to receive the food and drink. It is formed exactly like *ein haven bî dem fiure,* in which food is cooked. If the kettle is filled to excess, the contents become uncontrollable— they must boil over. Consequently, the food does not cook; or, it will burn and still not be cooked. By analogy this is exactly what happens in the stomach of the glutton. It must be remembered, he remarks, that the liver lies next to the stomach and supplies great heat which boils food in the stomach. Hence, unless a person is frugal in his eating habits, the food will boil over and cause the individual to become ill.

Berthold sees fit to discuss this topic at greater length, with the hope of discouraging over-indulgence in food and drink. By presenting an adequate description of the constituents of the human body, he opens the discussion with the question: " *Welchez ist daz hûsgesinde des libes?* To Berthold the parts are: veins, members, brain, blood, marrow, flesh, heart, and skeleton. From the stomach they receive nourishment and strength. When insufficient food is taken into the stomach, the veins and members from which the body gets its strength are not nourished, so the body becomes weak, and the person melancholy. Neverthelesss, it is better to have less

[147] Cf. I 103, 11 ff.

[148] The following material and citations appearing without footnote references are found: I 430-434 *passim.* Cf. also II 204-205.

than too much in the stomach, for the heat of the liver " will cook it "—and the stomach must neither " run over " nor " burn.'' Berthold mentions more ill effects of gluttony:

Und ist daz der mage übergêt, sô geraetet der überflusz etwenne gein dem houbete, daz dem menschen etewenne diu ôren vervallent, daz er ungehoernde wirt, oder für die gesiht, daz er erblindet oder sus boesiu ougen gewinnet, sûröuge oder glaseöuge oder starblint.   (I 430, 8 ff.)

Furthermore,

Geraetet es zwischen hût unde fleisch, sô wirdest dû wazzersühtic oder ûzsetzic oder gelsühtic oder sus als unflaetic daz dû dîr lange widerzaeme bist und andern liuten. Geraetet ez danne in daz geaeder, sô werdent dir die hende zitern. Geraetet ez dir danne in diu glider, sô wirdest dû lam oder betterisic.   (I 433, 16 ff.)

Gluttony likewise causes a burning in the stomach which ultimately produces consumption or recurring fevers. Many other sicknesses arise from gluttony which result in slow or sudden deaths.[149]

Berthold states another item which he considers of vast importance with reference to gluttony, viz., that very few children of the wealthy class reach adulthood or old age, while the children of the poor do. The reason Berthold gives is that the rich children are surfeited.[150] Wealthy parents over-feed their children, and cater to their fastidious appetites. Rich parents are under the false impression that they evidence love for their children by giving them more food than the children can take. Berthold laments the harm done by the lack of sobriety in eating. He pities the rich infant because:

Sô machet im diu swester ein muoselîn unde strîchet im eht în; sô ist sîn hevelîn klein, sîn megelîn, und ez ist vil schiere vol worden: sô püpelt ez im her wider ûz; sô strîchet eht sie dar. Sô kümt danne diu muome, diu tuot im daz selbe. Sô kümt danne diu amme unde sprichet: ' owê mîns kindes! daz enbeiz hiute nihtes.' Diu strîchet im danne als ie von êrste în. Sô weinet ez, sô zabelt ez.   (I 433, 32 ff.)

No wonder, then, that the children of the rich do not attain old

[149] For the signs of both bodily and spiritual death through gluttony, cf. I 515, 28-37.

[150] In another instance without reference to class distinction, Berthold says: " Einz daz einen becher kûme ze rehte erheben mac, daz wil nû ze dem wîne sitzen unde wil dâ schallen unde sneren unde trunken werden '' (I 469, 13 ff.).

age. Therefore, parents are warned to abandon these harmful sins if not for the good of their souls and their honor, and for God's sake, then at least for the sake of the health and long life of the children.[151]

On the Last Day, all gluttons must be judged and condemned by Almighty God and the heavenly armies; devils will drag them into hell with them.[152] There they shall have a " host " who will gorge them and satisfy their desires; but they can never be satisfied until they see Esau's shingle and shelter, under whose banner they will burn forever.[153] Gluttons rightfully merit damnation, because they are guilty of the most harmful and worst sin the world ever experienced; otherwise it would not be a capital sin.[154] This vice has manifold ramifications which harm many a family so that they will never prosper and will often be reduced to misery and poverty.[155] But before they reach this state, they shall have committed sins of impurity kindled by the heat of excess food, and robbed, and deceived, and lied; hence, they will be severely judged on the Last Day with sharp blows; and they must be damned eternally—first, the soul, and after Judgment Day, both soul and body.[156] Berthold reminds gluttons that they will be held accountable for every drink and every mouthful they take without necessity, for some gorge the stomach with what would suffice for ten persons.[157]

Berthold says he fears that many men do not want to combat this vice. However, if they do not wish to conquer gluttony for God's sake, then they should do it so that they may not be rejected scornfully by the whole world, or that they do not devour that which robs their children and wives of life.[158] To these he says bitterly:

Pfi, schantflec, daz hât dir allez samt dîn unmaezic munt verlorn und wirt dîn doch niemer rât. Ach, lecker, lecke în und giuz in dich, daz dû erküelest und daz ir daz fiur dâ ze helle deste baz erlîden muget.

(II 182, 10 ff.)

Furthermore, they are so unappreciative of the sufferings God endured through them, they refuse Him even slight honor by

---

[151] Cf. also II 16, 12 ff.

[152] Cf. I 190, 36 ff.

[153] Cf. I 261, 8 ff.

[154] Cf. I 191, 10-15 *passim.*

[155] Cf. *ibid.*, 17 ff.

[156] Cf. *ibid.*, 21 ff.

[157] Cf. I 469, 1 ff.

[158] Cf. II 182, 2 ff., 204, 14 ff.

abstaining from food and drink.[159] If they will not honor Our Lord because of His sufferings, then they should do so for their own honor, and for the good of their bodies, because gluttony not only deprives them of health and long life, but,

Ez nimt dir ouch guot und êre und alle dîn gewissen [160] daz dû und dîniu kint alwegen dester swecher und unsaeliger müezet sîn, ez bringt manigen darzuo daz er stilt oder roubet und denne erhangen oder er ertrenkt wirt.

(II 16, 18 ff.)

Formerly, women practiced temperance in food and drink, but now, Berthold says, it has become a custom that:

bis der man daz swert vertrinket, sô hât sie den snüerrinc unde daz houbettuoch vertrunken. (I 431, 33 ff.)

From the treatment accorded this capital sin, Berthold may be viewed as theologian and physician. Because gluttony makes the soul a slave to the body, it brutalizes man, and paves the way to unchastity. Over-indulgence in food does produce heat in the body which is apt to enkindle lust. Moreover he says also that it fosters a spirit of debauchery which weakens the will whilst it develops a love for sensual pleasure. Physicians, too, say that since food is necessary for life, it must be taken sanely in order to be conducive to long-life. They maintain also that sobriety or frugality is the essential condition of physical and moral vigor.[161]

Gluttony may go to such extremes that for a time, the guilty one will be incapacitated for the fulfillment of his duties of state, or for the compliance with divine and ecclesiastical laws, for example, when it injures health, and causes one to violate the laws of fast or abstinence.[162]

d. *Virtue Opposed to Gluttony: Temperance*

Gluttony should be overcome by the best of all virtues, temperance, which is most necessary for eternal life.[163] Berthold employs the example of Moses and Elias who went without food for thirty days; and Almighty God, also, who was even tempted by

---

[159] Cf. II 16, 8 ff.   [160] Cf. also II 101, 29 f.

[161] Cf. E. Caustier, *La vie et la santé* (Paris, 1904), 115.

[162] Cf. also St. Thomas, IIa IIae q. 148.

[163] Cf. I 103, 20 f., 561, 11.

the evil spirit to break His fast, but He said: " ganc hin, dû boeser sathanas! jâ sol man alleine niht des brôtes leben." [164] With these words Berthold says God showed that temperance is a virtue which directs one to the joys of eternal life, where he will be everlastingly nourished by the Beatific Vision, for God Himself said: " kumet her zuo mir, ich wil iuch spîsen." [165] Another illustration used by the preacher to encourage temperance is Lazarus, who was turned away from the rich man's door after he begged for the crumbs which fell from the table. Yet many now think they would cease to exist if they were not always filled like a " tart." [166]

If a person resemble God in this virtue, he will be assured of a high place in the promised land; but if he does not restrain the appetites of the body, he will never have the joy of seeing Our Lord.[167] And since gluttony has *manigerlei verdampnisse und schaden,* persons should fast.[168]

Berthold narrows the meaning of temperance to suit the virtue opposed to gluttony: fasting. Fasting is virtuous because it is an act which is ordained through reason to some honorable good. Such the act of fasting may be. It is done to repress carnal concupiscences (2 Cor. vi, 5); it is done that the mind may be more freely elevated to contemplate the most exalted things (Dan. x, 3); and also as a " satisfaction " for sins (Joel ii, 12).[169]

E. HATRED AND ENVY

The devil's leading apprentices, hatred and envy, have invested him with great power which he uses so adroitly, that persons in *all* states of life, whether rich or poor, fall ready victims to him.[170] Even in that particular congregation to which Berthold is speaking, he thinks there are very few who bear neither hatred nor envy against their neighbors.[171] He warns them that thousands have

---

[164] Cf. I 103, 23 ff.   [166] Cf. *ibid.,* 34 ff.
[165] Cf. *ibid.,* 28 ff.   [167] Cf. I 254, 34 ff.

[168] Cf. II 16, 22 f. Immediately following, Berthold discusses all the days on which persons are to fast. Cf. also *Catholic Encyclopedia,* I 68-69.

[169] Cf. St. Thomas, IIa IIae p. 148, a. 1; St. Augustine, Serm. De Orat. et Jejun., 230 De Temp.

[170] Cf. I 522, 34 ff.

[171] Cf. I 82, 3 ff.

been cast into the depths of hell through hatred and envy,[172] the sins which bear threefold fruit of depravity:

Daz ein: daz er den menschen verderbet an guotem gemüete, daz er gein gote und gein der werlte haben solte, wan in izzet der haz in dem herzen als der rost tuot îsen. Daz ander: daz er den menschen verdamnet an der sêle, wan ez der sünden einiu ist, dâ mite man verdampt wirt. Daz dritte: daz er den menschen ofte in grôze sünde wirft. (I 106, 17 ff.)

Berthold becomes severe when he tells the devil to garner those who are hateful and envious of heart, because they are misfits in the Kingdom of God.[173] For however small the possessions of those about them, they, in their malice, bear hatred and envy against them.[174] Hence, those people are inimical to God who are hateful and envious of those who have never harmed them but happen to be better situated.[175] There are persons who, out of hatred and envy, begrudge fellow-Christians if the latter have more friends, or property, or better fortune in business; or they may, for no reason, bear hatred and envy,[176] and wish them evil, and become jealous, and rejoice at their misfortunes.[177] They should not begrudge their neighbors for what God has granted them; or for what they have gained by honest work, or for what they have had since birth, or for what they have gained by less work—all which God in His wisdom, often turns into good.[178] Even though persons favored in the goods of this world cause others great sorrow, the latter ought not to bear hatred or envy against them, because they may but be tools in the hands of God to purge them from worldly dross.[179] Berthold calls upon all the Saints to use their powerful intercession, and to let it be known that they are loyal to Almighty God, and that they will deny help to all those who sin against Him, and that they will administer blows that will never heal, to each and everyone of them.[180] This is, of course, the grotesque language of the missionary Berthold.

[172] Cf. I 100, 14 f., also II 180, 32.
[173] Cf. I 464, 34 ff.   [174] Cf. *ibid.*, 37 f.   [175] Cf. *ibid.*, 39 f.
[176] Cf. I 187, 20 ff. Cf. also J. Mausbach, *op. cit.*, 111 f.
[177] Cf. II 101, 10 ff.
[178] Cf. I 465, 2 ff. Cf. also K. Hilgenreiner, *Lexikon für Theologie und Kirche* (Freiburg, 1932), Bd. IV, 837 f.
[179] Cf. I 187, 24 ff.
[180] Cf. *ibid.*, 27 ff. Here Berthold makes the saints in heaven guilty of

Berthold implores those who have been wanting in love towards
God and neighbor to drive away hatred and envy from their hearts,
and thereby avoid the awful curse, " *Verfluochet sî der sinem ebenkristen nît und haz treit.*" Then they will also evade other great
sins which hatred and envy engender: *mord, rouben, brennen.*[181]
Those who hate with a deadly hatred, and murder even though
only by desire, have already done so, and before God they are really
murderers.[182] To the *manslehtic,* Berthold says:

Wâ bist dû, Kâins bruoder, der sînen bruoder vor nîde unde vor hazze ze
tôde sluoc? Jâ haeten wir an den tiuveln hazzes unde nîdes genuoc.

(I 465, 28 ff.)

Therefore, the preacher entreats them again to cast from their
hearts these vices against their fellow-men even though their
neighbors may have caused them some grief by word and action.[183]
Notwithstanding the harm that may have been inflicted, the
guilty ones must be forgiven, so that God may be disposed also
to condone the frailties of the offended. Berthold reminds them of
the concluding words of the Lord's Prayer: "*unde vergip uns
unser schulde, als wir tuon unsern schuldigaeren.*" [184] Frequently,
in his treatment of hatred and envy, Berthold emphasizes the importance of forgiveness, so that God in turn may show mercy. He
tells the people to show mercy to their enemies even as the suffering
Jesus forgave His executioners.[185]

Hatred and envy dries up the body [186] and whoever harbors these
vices against one by whom he was never harmed, is committing an
inhuman sin.[187]   And even if a great injury has been inflicted, it is
not commensurable with the dignity of man to resort to reprisal; it
borders on the diabolical.[188] However strong, and even natural the
promptings to revenge for the hurt inflicted, nevertheless, even if
someone slew another's father and mother, and murdered his chil-

passions which cannot be reconciled with their sainthood. Undoubtedly,
he is here using highly figurative language to inculcate upon his hearers
the malice and perversity of sin.

[181] Cf. II 219, 15 ff.
[182] Cf. I 277, 30ff.
[183] Cf. *ibid.*, 34 ff., II 31, 21 ff.
[184] Cf. I 277, 37 ff., 278, 3 ff.
[185] Cf. I 28, 4 ff.
[186] Cf. I 465, 22 f.
[187] Cf. *ibid.*, 37 ff.
[188] Cf. *ibid.*, 39 f.

dren before his eyes—the latter must become the murderer's friend, otherwise he shall forfeit his soul.[189]

All evil arises from the promptings of the devils, and these in turn will spawn hatred and envy; the devils ever seek to increase the companions of their misery.[190] Berthold exclaims:

Nû seht, ir hêrschaft alle samt, wie des danne rât müge werden, der einem haz under nît treit, der im nie dehein leit getet? Nû seht, ir tiuvele, welh ein michel schar ir mir unde dem almehtigen gote dâ hin füeret in dem stricke, der dâ haz unde nît heizet! (I 466, 5 ff.)

Finally, he draws in lurid colors the last moments of the hateful and envious:

Swenne der arzât zuo dem siechen gêt unde . . . kêret sich danne der sieche gein der want unde siht die liute ungerne an, daz ist ein zeichen des tôdes an dem lîbe, unde . . . tôt an der sêle. Alle die sô nîdic unde sô hezzic sint, daz sie eht einz niht mügent an gesehen vor nîde unde vor hazze unde diu ougen ab im werfent vil nîtlîche unde vil hezzelîchen: dû bist tôtsiech an der sêle, unde wirdest dû dâ mite begriffen âne die heilige erzenîe, dû muost alse lange in der helle sîn, als got ein herre in himel ist. (I 513, 38 ff.)

The principal themes in this category (Hatred and Envy), are love of enemy, and the necessity of observing that precept of charity which likens man to God. In one way it is manifested by a special love for enemies on all occasions, according to the counsel of Our Lord: "Love your enemies: do good to them that hate you: etc." (Matt. v. 44).

The sort of hatred with which Berthold is concerned is commonly called *odium inimicitiae* by theologians. It aims directly at the person, indulges a propensity to see what is evil in him, feels a fierce satisfaction at anything tending to his discredit, and is keenly desirous that his lot may be an unmixedly hard one, either in a general or a specific way. This kind of *odium* may even prompt the sinner to loathe God, and to regret the Divine perfections in so far as they belong to God.[191] Hatred, a mental state of revulsion from something that offends, has the potency to intensify a desire to harm or destroy the object hated. Its consequences are

[189] Cf. I 466, 1 ff., II 180, 35 ff.
[190] Cf. I 465, 30 ff.
[191] Cf. *Catholic Encyclopedia*, VII, 149.

far-reaching and disastrous. It may let loose many of thè most malignant human passions such as retaliation and revenge. Hence, Berthold's references to murder. St. Thomas (IIa IIae q. 34, a. 5) does not count hatred among the capital sins because it is last, not first, in the order of destruction of what is virtuous to man; for it is most opposed to nature. Berthold is not wrong, however, in linking hatred with envy in his enumeration of the capital sins, for envy is sorrow at another's good; it follows that the good is rendered hateful to a person, and from envy springs hatred.

The *filiae* of envy with which Berthold is concerned are *exultatio in adversis* and *afflictio in prosperis*. These, of course, are hatred itself, because just as good which delights causes love, so does sorrow cause hatred.

e. Virtue opposed to Hatred and Envy: Love [192]

The whole world should embrace the virtue of love (*minne*), because it pleases God beyond measure; [193] it nourishes the soul, and strengthens the body against temptations, worldliness, desires of the flesh, and the counsels of the devil. [194] In contradistinction to the devil's apprentices, hatred and envy, love is depicted as a pure, all-virtuous and powerful virgin; and for her God died upon the cross. [195] In another instance Berthold portrays love as fire: everything thrown into fire, itself becomes fire, as when iron is consumed by fire, it also becomes fire. [196] So it is with love, and

Allez daz dem menschen iemer geschehen mac, daz die wâren minne hât, daz ist im allez ein minne. Hât ez grôz arbeit, daz ist im ouch ein minne; hât ez grôze armuot, ez ist im ein minne.   (I 545, 38 ff.)

Almighty God loves virtue above everything; but the best virtue is true love. [197] True love caused God to redeem us from eternal death through His death—no greater love has ever been manifested. Therefore God wishes that everyone attain true love which

---

[192] Cf. Keil, *op. cit.*, 25 ff. Cf. also Vol. II, Sermon LIII. For a good theological treatment of love, cf. A. Landgraf, *Lexikon für Theologie und Kirche*, Bd. VI, 558-562.

[193] Cf. I 453, 10 f.

[194] Cf. *ibid.*, 25 ff.

[195] Cf. I 523, 15 ff.

[196] Cf. I 545, 33 ff.

[197] Cf. I 100, 25, 28 ff.

dispells hatred, envy, and the multiple other vices. Berthold frequently tells his audiences that everyone should love God above all, with his whole heart, with his whole soul, with all his strength, and his fellow-Christian [198] as himself.[199] One should love God with his whole heart,

daz ist alsô gesprochen: daz dir nie friunt sô herzeliep enwart, dir sülle got noch lieber sîn, unde daz dû durch deheinen menschen niht tuon ensolt, ez sî dîn kint oder dîn hûsfrouwe . . . sô solt dû got sô herzeclîchen minnen, daz dû niemer dehein dinc solt getuon deheinem dînem friunde ze liebe daz wider got sî.   (I 166, 38 ff.)

And man should love God with his whole soul, and avoid sin out of love of God, not for fear of hell or punishment!

. . . daz dû alle toetlîche sünde mîden solt durch die *liebe* diu dû ze *gote* hâst alse flîzeclîchen als ob nie helle oder tiuvel worden waere; unde *niht* sô vil *durch die vorhte der helle*: noch mêr durch die liebe, die dû ze gote hâst danne durch dîne eigene sêle unde durch die vorhte, die dû zer helle hâst unde ze dem tiuvel unde ze der martel der helle.   (I 167, 7 ff.)

And with all his strength,

. . . daz dû got umb alle sîne genâde loben solt und êren unde minnen umb alle die genâde, die er an dir begangen hât und an allem menschlîchem künne.   (I 167, 14 ff.)

At this point, attention should be paid to Berthold's positive Christianity. He underscores an active, affirmative attitude: do good *not* because you *fear the devil*, but because you *love God*. Many scholars today accuse the medieval clergy of an exaggerated hostility to the world and its legitimate joys, or an entirely negative, scornful, scolding, condemning attitude toward man.

Speaking of false love, Berthold warns the people against " penny-preachers "—those priests who promise that they will absolve a sinner after payment of a fee—who sham the love of God, who deceive and impress with prayer, almsgiving, bowing before His images, or preaching about His love; but like Judas they lead thousands of souls to perdition. Berthold regrets that these hypocrites should have ever been born.[200] This, too, is an

[198] Berthold often varies this term with " neighbor."
[199] Cf. I 523, 19 ff., 30 ff.
[200] Cf. I 543, *passim.* Cf. I 61, 36 ff.

admirable and significant utterance of Berthold who was an honest friend of the people and their spiritual welfare. Love is the virtue that brought thousands of Saints to heaven. Mary Magdalen was purged of her sins because of her love; and the Blessed Mother forgave those who killed her holy, gentle and beloved Child before her very eyes. Her Son, too, forgave all those who murdered Him. Therefore everybody must forgive, regardless of the harm inflicted by his neighbor.[201]

The injunction, *daz dû dînen naehsten minnen solt alse dich selben,* according to Berthold, implies a twofold love of neighbor.[202] First, a person must love his neighbor in God, i. e., without violating the Commandments of God:

Daz ist alsô gesprochen, daz dû kein dinc tuon solt durch dekeinen dînen friunt daz wider got ist, weder roup noch brant . . . manslaht noch wunden noch nihtes niht. . . . Wan taetest duz durch dich selben, sô waerest dû dâ mite verlorn; tuost dû ez aber durch dînen friunt, sô bist dû noch baz verlorn. Dû solt im weder unkiusche noch keiner dinge die wider got sîn helfen.   (1 27, 11 ff.)

Secondly, he must love his neighbor for his own spiritual sake, through God:

Daz ist, daz dû im gunnen solt daz dû dir ganst êren unde guotes unde himelrîches, und im ergunnest daz dû dir selben ganst.

.   .   .   .

Und ist ez halt, daz er dir grôz herzeleit getân hât, dannoch soltû in minnen, alles durch got, daz dû im durch got allez . . . vergebest. . . .
                                                        (1 27, 29 ff.)

A member of the congregation interrupts the speaker to take exception to the injunction—that one should love his neighbor as himself; should bear neither hatred nor envy against him, and should wish his neighbor what he wishes for himself—by stating that the preacher himself does not execute this command.[203]

' Owê, bruoder Berhtolt, des tuost dû doch selber niht. Dû hâst guoter röcke zwêne unde sitzet manigez hie daz niwan einen hât, und ist der selbe vil boese, unde gizzest dir vil genuoc, unde gizze ich vil übel.' (1 544, 21 ff.)

Berthold's reply is subtle and naïve:

[201] Cf. I 252, 22 ff., 360, 9 ff.
[202] Cf. I 27, 6 f.   [203] Cf. I 544, 18 ff.

Daz ist vil wâr. Ich hân zwêne röcke an, ich gibe aber dir des einen niht: ich wolte aber gar gerne daz dû einen semelîchen haetest unde daz dû alse wol gaezest unde getrünkest alse ich. (1 544, 25 ff.)

Here Berthold explains that the true love in this instance lies in the sincere *wish* that his neighbor have the same.[204] If a person ought to give to another, when he had only a modicum more than the other, no one would be happy, and,

wer arbeitte danne daz die werlt hine kaeme? Ich hân zwêne röcke, gaebe ich dir der einen, sô haete ich ze wênic. Dû solt im des wol günnen, waz er êren unde guotes mêr hât danne dû, von friunden oder swâ von ez in ist an kumen. (1 544, 33 ff.)

One must love his neighbor in God as is shown in the Lord's Prayer:

Wan wir alle sprechen: 'vater unser' in dem pater noster . . . sô hât uns got erzöuget, daz wir alle geswistrîde sîn, unde süln daz tuon in gote unde süln alle einander liep haben. . . . (I 545, 6 ff.)

Berthold expatiates upon this by stressing the importance of forgiveness again. Irrespective of the harm done to a person by his neighbor—whether it be by curse, mockery, oppression, or theft— he must be forgiven for God's sake.[205]

With similar treatment, Berthold preaches of "peace" (*fride*) among neighbors [206] and peace with one's self.[207] He discusses the former with the slightly varied material [208] which he utilized in his expatiation of love of neighbor. Peace [209] with self is commanded by Almighty God and conveys the significance:

. . . daz der lîp sol mit der sêle vereinet sîn, daz der lîp niht begern sol swaz der sêle schade sî. Sô hâst dû fride mit dir selbe. (I 240, 24 ff.)

Berthold speaks of "loving our neighbor for God's sake." The expression means that a person rise above the consideration of mere natural solidarity and fellow-feeling to the higher view of our common Divine adoption and heavenly heritage. God is loved

[204] Cf. *ibid.*, 28 f.
[205] Cf. I 545, *passim.* Cf. II 236, 35 ff.
[206] Cf. I 238, 34 f.
[207] Cf. I 240, 24.
[208] Cf. I 238-239.
[209] Berthold defines peace: I 236, 21 ff.

in our neighbor, but our neighbor has not that goodness which is the ground of love essentially, but only by participation.[210]

Berthold's explanation of true love as "lying in the *sincere wish* that his neighbor have the same," seems to be a rather disputed question. Müller [211] maintains that there is never any obligation of using the necessities of life for almsgiving, because well-regulated charity ordinarily obliges everyone to prefer his own vital interests to those of his neighbor. St. Thomas [212] holds that to a neighbor in extreme indigence relief must be ministered by using such commodities as are superfluous to vital interests, even though such should be required for social advantages. Suarez [213] says that charity demands that the vital interests of an indigent neighbor should supersede personal advantages of a much lower order. The transgression of this obligation involves a mortal sin. Nevertheless, he says [214] no one, however wealthy, is obliged to take extraordinary measures to assist a neighbor even in direful straits, e. g., a wealthy citizen is not bound to send a dying pauper to a more salubrious clime. Theologians holding that the obligation is serious, seem to espouse a cause in harmony with the teaching of Scripture and the authority of the Fathers.[215]

F. ANGER

Another wicked, shameless vassal of the devil, empowered by him to force thousands of persons into his service, is anger, one of the causes of all vices since it is one of the seven capital sins.[216] Anger searches out, and executes great crimes through the many individuals who allow themselves to be allied with it, and it also does one immeasurable harm.[217] In one sermon Berthold enumerates *drier hande schaden*:

[210] Cf. St. Thomas Aquinas, IIa IIae q. 26, a. 3.

[211] Cf. *Theologia Moralis* (Vindobonae, 1873), II 112, § 30.

[212] Cf. IIa IIae q. 32, a. 6.

[213] Cf. "De Charitate, Disput." vii, § 4, No. 3, *Opera Omnia* (Parisiis, 1878).

[214] Cf. *loc. cit.*, § 4, No. 4.

[215] Cf. *Catholic Encyclopedia*, I 329.

[216] Cf. I 523, 38 ff.

[217] Cf. I 524, 4 ff. Cf. also *Lexikon für Theologie und Kirche*, Bd. X, 1093, as discussed by J. Mayer.

Daz ein daz ist, daz er den lîp verderbet. Etelîche werdent vergihtic vor zorne, etelîche anders sühtic. Daz ander: daz dir die liute gehaz unde vînt werdent: den dû niemer dehein leit getuost, die werdent dir vînt unde gehaz, die an dir sehent oder von dir hoerent sagen. 'Wech!' sprichet ieglîcher, 'ist daz der ungezogen . . . unde der sô unbescheiden?' . . . Der dritte schade unde der groeste: daz dir got selber vînt wirt und allez himelische her. (I 106, 37 ff.)

And in another sermon he says that the person who inclines to anger is bitter as gall, the bitterest of bitters, which makes this one a murderer, that one a robber, and still another a traitor who would deprive a person of his honor and possessions, and even of body and soul.[218]

Bitterness of heart through anger leads some to become *mortbeter*; others to become slanderers. In addition, many murder their wives: it is not uncommon that men beat their wives beyond recovery; and if they do not die immediately, death may come within six months—which otherwise would not happen. Again, others will bear the guilt when, out of anger, they beat their wives who are with child. In turn, this angers the wives and they chide and curse; consequently, there is never peace or reconciliation, or loyalty among them.[219] Furthermore, those who become so angry that they murder their neighbors, commit one of the four sins that cries to heaven for vengeance.[220] Moreover, besides being condemned by God, those who have thus sinned demolish their own lives, and they never reach a good age, for their bodies and souls will be crying to heaven for vengeance, and thus

. . . richet sie got selber an lîbe und an sêle. Sich, zürner, morder, bluottrinker, in der sünden bist dû einer, die dâ sô ruofent über lîp und über sêle. Ir tiuvele, seht, die habet iu alle samt unde füeret sie hin abe an den grunt der hellen zuo Herôdes dem zornigen unde zuo andern sînen genôzen, die ouch mit zorne der tiuvele genôzen worden sint unde die grisgrament sam ein lewe . . . sô in einer ein wörtelîn sprichet oder sô im ein halm twerhes in dem wege lît. (I 466, 24 ff.)

Anger usurps one of all one's honor, and is such a powerful vice that many go to their deaths from it.[221] And when the devil realizes that he is about to lose a human being, he becomes persistent and strikes and slays, and even if he were to be offered a

[218] Cf. I 189, 15 ff.
[219] Cf. *ibid.*, 24 ff.
[220] Cf. I 466, 17 ff.
[221] Cf. I 524, 10 ff.

5

kingdom in exchange, indeed, even heaven, he would not desist from his anger.[222]

This vice has led thousands of souls to hell; and for the most part, he condemns poor people for this sin.[223] They become irritable and quarrel over trifles or nothing at all; and should the slightest obstacle lie in their paths, they growl, rage, and curse as if possessed by the devil.[224] The elite are ashamed of such coarse and crude demeanor; however, when they become guilty of anger, they are responsible for greater evils, for through their uncontrolled passion many may become widows and orphans.[225]

God has no need of, nor does He even wish to see in His kingdom, those who out of anger, curse, swear, rage, and gnash their teeth as if they could not otherwise revenge themselves.[226] Nor does God want those who fling or dash to shards whatever happens to be close by, or those who tear into shreds their clothing, or that of their wives; or those who injure their constitutions by intemperate outbursts.[227]

As a *passion,* anger is a violent reaction caused by physical or moral suffering or annoyance. This vexation excites a violent emotion which arouses one's energies to overcome the difficulty. As a *sentiment,* anger consists in a vehement desire to repeal and punish an aggressor. Under certain conditions that anger (sentiment) may be legitimate.[228]

Anger as a capital vice is a violent and inordinate desire of punishing others; often it is accompanied by hatred which seeks not merely to repel aggression but to take revenge. Such a sentiment is more deliberate, more lasting, and has, therefore, more serious consequences. Anger at first, consists in a mere impulse of *impatience,* followed by *agitation* which manifests dissatisfaction by uncontrolled gestures; then it reaches the stage of *violence,* often culminating in temporary insanity. Hence, it is clearly seen why Berthold refers to murder and other actrocities in this category.

[222] Cf. *ibid.,* 12 ff.
[223] Cf. I 101, 1 ff.
[224] Cf. *ibid.,* 8 ff., II 179, 31 ff.
[225] Cf. I 101, 4 ff.
[226] Cf. I 466, 10 ff.
[227] Cf. *ibid.,* 14 ff.
[228] Cf. Tanquerey, *op. cit.,* II 407 f.

f. Virtue Opposed to Anger: Patience

Anger must be combatted, according to Berthold, with the virtue of patience, one of the seven greatest virtues by which many Saints entered the Kingdom of God. Therefore, all those persons eager to gain heaven must have practiced patience and the other six virtues. Our Blessed Lady possessed the virtue of patience beyond measure; and it was through patience that many other Saints attained heaven.

Berthold cautions the people that they patiently bear whatever torments they have of soul, body, of possessions, or from infirmities of poverty. He teaches them further that they must bear misfortunes patiently like Job, who pleased God more than any other person living during his time. In contrast, the preacher says it should never be that, for instance, if a dish is upset, some men want to choke their wives or their children. This enrages the wife and she nags at her husband until he takes her by the hair and drags her from place to place, and steps on her head, as if wanting to break her neck. Those who storm and rage through anger, will not share the dwelling which God created and chose for His people and angels, because this vice is one of the seven that leads people away from the joy of Our Lord. And those who die with this sin must remain in hell and burn with the devil as long as God is in heaven.[229]

People should remember all the sufferings that God patiently underwent for their sake. Even when the persecutors spat upon His noble countenance, He bore all patiently.[230] And innocent that He was, He did not become angry; He endured it like a little lamb.[231]

Here Berthold presents Christ as the model after whom man, out of appreciation for His sufferings, ought to pattern himself. Great patience is exemplified in two ways: either when one suffers intensely in all patience, or when one suffers that which he could avoid if he so wished. From some of the examples of "impatience" which Berthold employs, he could have had in mind the words of the Gospel: "when He suffered, He threatened not" (I Pet., ii, 23).

[229] The foregoing material is found: I 101 f.
[230] Cf. I 254, 7 ff.   [231] Cf. I 524, 33 f.

G. SLOTH [232]

A great number of persons sin against God with this vice: [233] some are too indolent to go to Church, or say one " Our Father," others to listen to sermons; some are too indolent to give alms, others to gain an indulgence; and some are too indolent to remain in Church even for a short time with due propriety while services are in progress: they grumble and mock as if they were at the market place—and their bodies and souls shall be condemned to hell.[234] They demonstrate sloth toward that with which they ought to serve God, yet they are all too prompt to arrive at sensual pleasures, story-telling, and acting silly.[235]

Young and old, rich and poor, are ensnared with this vice. Some are so slothful they would not enter the nearest Church if it were not that people would talk.[236] The speaker says there are many in his audience who have not seen the interior of a Church for six months, and such persons are not to be regarded as Christians. Christians ought to say sixty or seventy Our Fathers every day. Instead, there are many who do not even bless themselves upon arising in the morning, and cannot even recite the Lord's Prayer until they are twenty years old, because they were too indolent. All those who reach the age of fourteen years, and die without knowing the Lord's Prayer, are to be buried in the potter's field.[327] Berthold laments the fact that the slothful should have ever been born, because in later life they become so negligent and calloused against serving God, and granting Him honor by assisting at Mass. There are many who ward off everything but indolence and ill-will so that they do not even favor themselves with the blessings of Mass, or favor God with honor by assisting at Mass everyday.[238] The devil has every right to claim for himself those who are slothful in serving God.[239]

Since God allowed Himself to be crucified for all sinners, and suffered bitter agony to serve mankind, God will not dispense mankind from the obligation of serving Him.[240] Since God created all

---

[232] Berthold always refers to this vice as: " Trâkheit *an gotes dienste.*"

[233] Cf. I 189, 39 f.

[234] Cf. I 102, 6 ff., 466, 34 ff.

[235] Cf. II 180, 14 ff.

[236] Cf. I 525, 1 ff.

[237] Cf. I 467, 2 ff.

[238] Cf. I 494, 18 ff.

[239] Cf. I 466, 32 f.

[240] Cf. I 190, 2 ff.

things for the benefit and for the service of mankind, and God
Himself serves and has served man, it is reasonable and fair that
man in turn serve God with his whole heart.[241] Although God
wants man to serve Him, He does not expect such great service as
He did formerly, when the "way of martyrdom" was open to
reach heaven. Berthold warns his hearers, however, that this way
will be re-opened before Judgment Day, when the Antichrist comes,
and that they should rather suffer tortures than lose their Christian faith.[242] Therefore, like grasshoppers, they should ever be
quick, and not lazy to serve God.[243]

Parents who are slothful in rearing their children shall be held
guilty for all the misdeeds the latter perform.[244] Among the thousands of souls lost because they encourage laziness in serving God
are especially manufacturers of dice.[245]

Although He never suffered for them, Angels serve God willingly
and promptly; hence man is indebted to God a thousand times more
than Angels. Therefore he must be ever willing and prompt to
serve God, and not serve Him grudgingly, lazily, or as if he were
bored.[246]

The spiritual sloth which Berthold treats consists in a species
of dislike for things spiritual, which tends to make a person negligent in the performance of his exercises of piety, causes him to
shorten them or to omit them altogether on the slightest pretext.
The individual contrives to escape any exertion that might inter-
fere with his comfort or involve fatigue.[247]

If sloth makes the friendship of God tedious and irksome because of the trouble it takes to preserve it, it is a mortal sin,
inasmuch as it is directly against our obligation of loving God with
our whole heart.[248]

g. Virtue opposed to Sloth: Diligence

Berthold exhorts the populace to be prompt and diligent in every
way—*almuosen ze gebenne unde beten unde wachen unde vasten*

[241] Cf. *ibid.*, 5 ff.
[242] Cf. I 525, 3 ff.
[243] Cf. I 559, 30 ff.
[244] Cf. I 36, 29 ff.
[245] Cf. I 15, 2 ff.
[246] Cf. I 559, 34 ff.
[247] Cf. Tanquerey, *op. cit.*, II 562 f.
[248] T. Slater, S. J., *A Manual of Moral Theology* (New York, and Chicago, 1908), I 161.

*gote ze dienste unde villât ze nemenne unde gehôrsamkeit ze hal-
tenne unde zuo predigen ze gênne unde ze antlâzen*—like many
Saints who possess the Kingdom of Heaven, and who never grew
tired of the many great works which they suffered out of love for
Our Lord.[249] The people are reminded of Saints Stephen, Lawrence,
Gregory, and Saints Margaret and Juliana who were never slothful
to suffer horrible pain and inhuman torture.[250]

Berthold likens diligence in serving God to a virgin, the mother
of all virtues; for whoever serves God willingly is an enemy of sin.
Thus, all service which one may render God could not be dearer to
Him, than that type of service which makes one hate sin.[251]

To the objection of some people in Berthold's audience that they
have more to do than pray all day long and go to Church, Berthold
explains that God does not expect that of His people. On the other
hand, God demands that they execute every duty of their state in
life. God has given each person a duty in which he must serve
Him: one, for the good of his body; the other for the good of his
soul. Whether the person be priest or layman, judge or knight,
merchant or farmer, he must be loyal, honest, and obedient to his
office.[252] Religious and widows, whether they be in cloisters or not,

sô sulnt sie vil gebeten unde ᴧweinen unde sulnt aller guoten dinge vil
durch got üeben an in selben.   (I 255, 28 ff.)

This, of course, is not expected of married people. Nevertheless,
they too, must render their share of worship to honor, entreat, and
thank God that they may remain free from sin, and perform the
duties of their state in life.[253] Since on the Last Day they will be
especially asked, the rich must have performed all the Corporal
Works of Mercy.[254] Berthold states what is expected of people in
general:

Sehs unde sibenzic pater noster dâ ist ein ieglîcher mensche mit enbrosten.
Der aber mêr mac, der sol ouch mêr tuon. Die aber staeteclîchen müezent
wirken, die beten nâch ir staten als sie got ermane. Und alle die got

[249] Cf. I 102, 19 ff.
[250] Cf. *ibid.*, 26 ff.
[251] Cf. I 525, 13 ff.
[252] Cf. I 255, 18 ff.
[253] Cf. *ibid.*, 30 ff.
[254] Cf. I 190, 12 ff.

lazlîchen dienent unde gerner fluochent unde scheltent danne daz sie ein pater noster sprechen, die tuont vil rehte als ir herre der tiuvel, wan der geriet ouch niht guotes.　(I 255, 33 ff.)

Nevertheless, Berthold seems to become comparatively mild and says that he does not want the people to suffer such terrible tortures as the martyrs did. He declares that he does not wish more than that they flee from and avoid mortal sin.[255] And,

swâ ir daz übersehen habet, daz sult ir frumeclîchen büezen. . . . Unde dû solt ze deheinen dingen sô snel sîn als ze buoze. . . . Und . . . als iuch der almehtige got frâgende werde an dem jungesten tage: ' habet ir mir den hungrigen z'ezzen geben etc.,' daz er danne froelîche sprechen müge: ' kumt her, mîne erwelten, in daz rîche mînes vater. . . .' (I 102, 34 ff.)

Finally Berthold says of mortal sin:

. . . ich möhte die houbetsünde in fünf predigen niemer genennen, ob ich anders niht taete wan daz ich spraeche: dáz ist ein sünde, daz ist ouch ein houbetsünde, daz ist aber ein ander houbetsünde.　(I 429, 28 ff.)

The gloomy picture receives lighter tones, however, from his frequent and ever recurring statement:

Buoze nim ich all zît ûz.

Man is master of his acts through reason and free will, so he may choose to act or not to act says Berthold. Since every power is directed to its appropriate object, and the object of the will is some end, some good, it is evident that human acts are for the attainment of some end. So it is clearly seen that the important thought lying behind Berthold's treatment of Diligence is the performance of good with a supernatural motive in mind. Furthermore, he is stressing the fact that, while acts are voluntary, man should strive for activity offered ultimately for the attainment of spiritual benefit, and out of love for God.

[255] Cf. I 102, 31 ff.

CHAPTER II

SINS AGAINST THE FIRST THREE COMMANDMENTS

There is probably no document which has exercised a greater influence upon religious and mortal life than the Decalogue. On account of its brevity, its comprehensiveness, its forcefulness, and its limitations which lie simply on the surface, it has stood out from other teaching and has been embedded in Christian doctrine so that it is difficult for any Christian to escape knowledge of its contents.

The Decalogue comes to us by Revelation. There are two scriptural versions; one, in common use, being in Exodus xx, 2-17, the other in Deuteronomy v, 6-21. The "Ten Words" were given to the Jewish people through Moses, and were confirmed by Christ in the New Dispensation, which is the law of the shadow of things to come (Col. 2, 17). The ceremonial precepts of the Old Law are displaced once for all; for the Jewish Sabbath the Christian Church has substituted Sunday as the Lord's day, in memory of Christ's Resurrection.

Man's duties according to Natural Law are summarized in explicit terms in the Decalogue. The first three precepts refer to the external worship of God, the last seven refer to authority in the family, the sacredness of life and good report, the sanctity of marriage, and the right of property respectively.

Since these precepts are imposed by God, their observance is *prima facie* a matter of serious obligation. If they are violated in trivial matters—where from the nature of the case that is possible, as in the precept against theft—such violation is not a grave sin. It is the task of Moral Theology to try to distinguish between what is objectively serious and what is not, for there is an objective order to be maintained; subjectivism in morality leads to agnosticism or moral anarchy.[1]

The Decalogue often provided a basis for Berthold's homiletic examination—exhortation—and—application. Therefore it seems advisable to include, at this point, his own enumeration and

---

[1] Cf. H. Davis, S. J., *Moral and Pastoral Theology* (London, 1938), I 1.

54

arrangement. Because the following discussion is dependent upon them for clarity, it is important to note the subdivisions Berthold employs. All the sins, whether of omission or commission of which a man in the Middle Ages might be guilty, are discernible in the light of Berthold's summary. The Decalogue contains more moral doctrine than is expressed in the short formula under which it has come to us. In a figurative sense, the Divine precepts are considered as ten *helbelinge* which a soul must return in full to Almighty God at death. Inability to fully comply therewith, implies the loss of eternal salvation.

A. THE FIRST COMMANDMENT [2]

Part I

The first subdivision of the primary commandment *dû solt dekeinen fremeden got ane beten vor mir,* is *dû solt deheinen got ane beten danne mich, weder in dem himel noch ûf der erden noch under der erden.* This implies especially a censure against superstition.

a. Superstition

Berthold describes several superstitions [3] of the day as ways of breaking the first commandment, and, of incurring resultant spiritual death.

Sô geloubent etelîche an boesen aneganc: [4] daz ein wolf [5] guoten aneganc habe, der aller der werlte schaden tuot, und ist halt sô unreine daz

---

[2] The treatment of the precepts and their sub-parts will follow the series in which they are presented by Berthold. Since the Ten Commandments are discussed in Volume I, Sermon XIX, and Volume II, Sermon LVI, all material appearing without footnote references will be found in the above sermons. References and comments made on this material will bear the asterisk. In all cases where unasterisked footnotes occur in the following chapters, the material is that which has been gleaned and included to follow the outline resembling the divisions found in Aertnys-Danen, C.SS.R., *Theologia Moralis secundum doctrinam S. Alphonsi De Ligorio* (Turin, 1928), Tomus I.

[3] Cf. also Keil, *Sitte und Sittlichkeit,* § 44.

[4] Cf. J. Grimm, Deutsche Mythologie (Göttingen, 1854), II 1072 ff.

[5] For the parts that the wolf and other animals play in medieval superstition, cf. H. B. Schindler, *Der Aberglaube des Mittelalters,* 28 f.; cf. also

er die liute an stinket, daz nieman bî im genesen mac; unde daz ein gewîhter priester ⁶* boesen aneganc habe, an dem aller geloube lît: wan in hât got über alle menschen erhoehet. . . . Sô geloubent etelîche an boese hantgift.⁷* Sô gênt etelîche mit boesen batônjen ⁸* umbe unde mit boesem zouberlehe umbe, daz sie waenent eines gebûren sun oder einen kneht bezoubern. . . . Sô geloubent etelîche an den miusearn. Sô ist dem der hase übern wec geloufen.

In his discussions upon this vice, the preacher directs the majority of his vehement invectives to women. It is remarkable, in fact, that through these evil practices of women, men do not become *ûzsetzic* ⁹ or *unsinnic* . . . *von dem unbilde, daz die frouwen an iuch legent mit zouber;* ¹⁰ which, of course, occasions these women to condemn their souls.¹¹ Berthold expresses his disgust that women cast spells so that they may win the affection of a man.¹² He inquires acrimoniously of these *toerinne* why they limit their charms to the son of a farmer, or his servant; perhaps if they enchanted kings, they could become queens.¹³ Women utilize these vicious practices further:

C. Meyer, *Der Aberglaube des Mittelalters* (Basel, 1884), 224 f.; and E. Nussbaum, *Metapher und Gleichnis bei Berthold von Regensburg*, Diss. (Wien, 1902), 33-40.

⁶ The pagan superstition still flourished in Berthold's time which held it an evil omen to meet a priest the first thing in the morning. Cf. G. Coulton, "A Revivalist of Six Centuries Ago," in *North American Review*, CLXXXVI—1907, 277.

⁷ " Dieser Aberglaube ist noch heute in manchen Gegenden verbreitet. Hat jemand eine Krankheit, so kauft er einen neuen Topf oder ein neues Glas, ohne dabei zu feilschen. In dieses Gefäss zaubert er dann seine Krankheit durch Bestreichen hinein, legt dazu möglichst etwas vom kranken Glied, z. B. ein Haar oder . . . Fingernagel. Dann setzt er das Gefäss auf dem Weg aus. Wer nun den Topf nimmt, auf den geht die Krankheit über. Darum muss man um ihn einen grosssen Bogen machen. Eine andere Handgift ist freilich gut, wenn nämlich jemand auf dem Markt ein Handgeld von einer jungen Person erhalten hat." Keil, *op. cit.*, 186.

⁸ Concerning this, and other plants, cf. Meyer, *op. cit.*, 60 ff. Berthold mentions herbs again: II 70, 1; 147, 27. Cf. Nussbaum, *op. cit.*, 40 ff.

⁹ Cf. II 71, 9 f.   ¹⁰ I 464, 21 ff.   ¹¹ Cf. II 18, 34.

¹² Cf. II 70, 35 f. "Pfî geloubestû daz dû einem man sîn herze ûz sînem lîbe nemest und im ein strô hin wider stôzest? Sich, dû kanst borwol niemer ein reht ende nemen von dînem ungelouben, den dû trîbest mit zouberîe (II 70, 10 ff.). Cf. Meyer, *op. cit.*, 263.

¹³ Cf. II 70, 36 ff.; I 265, 2 f.

Sie zoubert, ê daz kint geboren wirt. Sie zoubert vor dem toufe . . . nâch dem toufe.[14] Nû sich, dû gewinnest dînem kinde, daz ez iemer deste arbeitsaeliger sîn muoz von dîme zoubern.　　　　　　　(II 71, 6 ff.)

The *zouberaerinnen* are severely rebuked for their sorcerous bewitchings, and are warned that they shall be damned for the spells they think they cast with toads and wild apples; nevertheless, those who bear guilt of the greatest of all sins—when charms are executed with the Host [15]—make themselves the devil's chosen people whom he will reward with a place of honor in the depths of hell.[16] Moreover, Berthold adds that if it were not for God's goodness and mercy, he would not be surprised,

. . . daz dich diu erde niht verslindet unde daz dich daz wilde fiwer niht verslindet . . . oder der donre niht ersleht. Jâ ist ez dir ze vil, daz dû mit andern dingen zouberst, daz halt gar lîhte unde gar boese ist; ich wil es geswîgen daz dû mit gote selben zouberst, daz dû im sô getân leit an im selben tuost. . . . Vil wunderlîchen balde in starke buoze, ê daz dich der donre slahe oder einen andern unrehten tôt nemest.　　　　(I 454, 18 ff.)

Besides using the Host, and toads, they perform superstitious actions with *heiligen krismen*, and with *totengebeine*, which, according to Berthold, is the worst of all sins against nature.[17] Furthermore, they sin against the Sacrament of Baptism:

. . . man sol niht toufen danne ein lebendigez kint oder einen lebendigen menschen, noch tôtez mensche noch tôtez gebeine noch silber noch golt noch wahs. . . . Pfî zouberaerinne, dînes atzemannes! [18] Waenest dû dem almehtigen gote sîne erzenîe velschen? Dû hast dich selben verdampt in daz êwige fiwer.　　　　　　　　　　　　　　　　(I 298, 22 ff.)

All classes of workers are reminded that unless they abandon their superstitious practices, they will be among the thousands who lose their souls through this sin.[19] Peasants do not escape the preacher's attention. They are addressed directly:

Owê, ir dorfliute, iuwer kaeme vil ze himele, wan daz selbe extlîn, daz ermordet alle, die an zouberîe geloubent und an wârsagen [20] und an wâr-

---

[14] Such practices are still prevalent among country-folk in certain regions of Italy.

[15] The Host, holy oils, and the water in the font had to be kept under lock and key from the common people who used them as engines of sorcery. cf. Coulton, *loc. cit.*, 281; cf. Meyer, *op. cit.*, 183 f.

[16] Cf. I 206, 19 ff.; 28 ff.　　　　　　　　[18] Cf. Grimm, *op. cit.*, 1045 ff.

[17] Cf. II 147, 25 ff.　　　　　　　　　　　[19] Cf. II 18, 28 ff.

sagerinne und an lüppelerinne, an nahtfrouwen und an sô getân gespüc und an pilwiz. Und etelîche geloubent an heilige brunnen, sô an heilige boume, sô an heilige greber ûf dem velde.   (II 70, 28 ff.)

Lastly, then, Berthold admits that superstitions are so numerous, "daz sîn nieman ze ende komen mac."

b. Idolatry

Berthold merely touches upon this by instructing the congregation against pagan forms of worship such as those practiced by the Babylonians who prayed to the sun, moon, and stars; the Greeks who prayed to human beings and to beasts, and the Egyptians who invoked the aid of the sea monster.[21]

Part II of First Commandment

The second part of the first commandment is: *daz dû âne val-scheit und âne hinderliste mit guoten triuwen an got geloubest unde swaz dû ze rehte von gote gelouben solt unde daz dîn kristen-geloube seit.*

Here Berthold's treatment is certainly far removed from the present-day interpretation. His injunction which appears in the following citation would receive scant consideration to-day:

Dû solt niht ze vil unde ze tiefe gedenken in dîme heiligen kristenglouben, wie dem unde dem sî unde wie daz unde daz gesîn müge, unde wie daz gesîn müge daz ein priester, der selbe in sünden ist, dich von dînen sünden müge enbinden.[22]*

He says that a priest's being able to absolve from sin while he himself is in state of sin should not be a source of wonder to his hearers, because even if a priest does not lead a holy life, the ordination to the priesthood is more than holy, for it is one of the seven Sacraments which Christ instituted on earth. To emphasize the unwisdom of this type of inquiry, Berthold effects an interest-

[20] Cf. Schindler, *op. cit.*, 209 f.
[21] Cf. A. Schaefer, *Die Verwandlung der menschlichen Gestalt im Volks-aberglauben* (Darmstadt, 1905), 51 ff.
[22] Elsewhere Berthold says: " . . . swer dâ giht, daz ein priester, der selbe in houbetsünden ist, daz der nieman von sînen sünden enbinden müge, der ist ouch ein ketzer " (I 406, 22 ff.).

ing comparison of the Christian faith to the sun, and further elaborates it:

Ez enhât nieman sô starkiu ougen, unde wil er ze lange unde ze vaste in die sunne und in daz brehende rat der sunnen sehen, er wirt als unmâzen kranc an sînen ougen, daz erz niemer überwindet; . . . Ze gelîcher wîse sol nieman ze vaste in den rehten kristengelouben sehen, anders er wirt sô kranc an dem gelouben, daz erz niemer überwindet, oder er wirt aber gar ze einem ketzer.

c. Heresy [23]

The treatment accorded heresy deals, in greater part, with the diabolical operations of heretics, and with Berthold's preoccupation of familiarizing the people therewith; and hence at the same time, instructing them accordingly so as to safeguard their Christian faith. The only theological dogma with which the preacher is concerned is Transubstantiation.

Sô nimt die ketzer unde die jüden wunder, wie daz gesîn müge, daz got gewandelt werde in ein brôt. Pfî, verfluochter ketzer unde stinkender jüde! Jâ hât der almehtige got hiute als grôze kraft, als dô er daz firmamente machte mit éinem worte. . . . Den gewalt hât er noch, daz er den heiligen worten die kraft gît, diu der priester drobe sprichet ob der materien, daz sich got wandelt, in daz brôt unde sîn heiligez bluot in den wîn.   (I 302, 22 ff.) [24]

Of heretics in general, Berthold says they are all those who believe *unglîch und reht wider got,* and

ez sint kristenliute gewesen, unde den glouben den sie gote geheizen in dem heiligen toufe, des sint sie aptrünnic worden unde sint gevallen ûz dem himelrîche der heiligen kristenheit (wan diu heilige kristenheit glîchet sich dem himelrîche) : dâ sint sie ûz gevallen von ir genôzen . . . als die tiuvel . . . aptrünnic wurden unde vielen in die verdampnisse. . . . Und als wênic daz die tiuvel willen hant daz sie iemer wider ze engeln werden, als wênic habent die ketzer willen daz sie iemer mêre kristenliute werden wider als ê.   (I 436, 37 ff.)

---

[23] " Die beiden neugegründeten Orden der Dominikaner und der Franciskaner waren zur Bekämpfung der Irrelehre berufen: die *constitutio contra haereticos* 1224 von Friedrich II sagt: ' Notum esse volumus fratres praedicatores et minores pro fidei negotio in partibus nostra haereticos deputatos.' " Wieser, *Berthold von Regensburg,* 21. Berthold is especially energetic in combatting heresy. Cf. E. Michael, *Kulturzustände des deutschen Volkes während des dreizehten Jahrhunderts* (Freiburg im Br., 1889), Zweites Buch, 173.

[24] Cf. also II 88, 8-28.

Heretics are forever at peace with the devil, for in two major respects they are identical:

Daz ein . . . das ist, daz er alle die er mac von gote kêret, daz er daz tuot, Wan er daz· himelrîche verworht unde verlorn hât, sô saehe er âne mâze gerne, daz er alle verworhten, die von Adâmes künne geborn sint, und er schüpfet unde raetet mit allem flîze, swie er kan unde mac, daz ir vil sî die den fride unsers herren zerbrechen. . . . Daz ander . . . daz ist, daz er sich niemer bekêren wil.[25]   (I 242, 12 ff.)

Since heretics are renegades of the Christian faith, their chief aim is to convert holy Christians to their beliefs. Therefore, persons should be vigilant because the heretic approaches by cunning to teach his doctrines. Also he will teach seemingly good things to lead the Christian astray; therefore the Christian must never wish to listen merely from curiosity. However, should the Christian listen to all the heretic has to say, the former has already been converted by the heretic in that the Christian's faith will become worse, weaker and weaker, and soon he will fall from the Society of Christians and thereby deprive himself of heaven and the Beatific Vision.[26] Furthermore, the heretic will appear as a priest to the people and will speak sweet, convincing words; he will perform exactly like a cat,[27] and will pollute people's bodies. He will speak of God and of angels; any human being would swear a thousand oaths he were an angel, instead of the devil himself.[28] Then he will say to a person that:

. . . er welle dich einen engel lâzen sehen unde welle dich lêren, daz dû got lîplîchen sehest, unde seit dir des sô vil vor, daz er dich schiere von dem kristenglouben hât gescheiden und daz dîn niemer rât wirt.
                                            (I 403, 14 ff.)

Again at length, Berthold discusses the ways of heretics. His

[25] " Wan er ist als gar verhertet unde versteinet als der tiuvel in der ketzerîe. Unde rehte als der kristalle von wazzer ze steine worden ist, als ist der ketzer von einem kristenmenschen worden. Und als wênic als man den kristallen iemer ze wazzer gemachen mac, als wênic mac man den ketzer iemer mêr ze einem kristenmenschen gemachen, er sî denne kürzlîche in die ketzerîe komen " (I 243, 7 ff.).

[26] Cf. I 242, 24 ff.; cf. II 77, 27 ff.

[27] The frequently quoted, interesting comparison of heretics with cats; of Berthold's play on the words *ketzer, katze,* cf. I 402, 19 ff.

[28] Cf. I 403, 7 ff.

purpose is once more to acquaint the people so they may avoid the irreligious, heretical doctrines, and have a firmer Christian faith. One item he particularly emphasizes is that heretics prey upon simple people in some corner; they avoid preaching in the open by day-light.[29] When these people are approached by heretics, Berthold instructs them that they should keep silence, and notify the parish priest who in turn is to deliver the heretics to the *werlte rihter unz an den bischof.*[30] Berthold cautions peasants especially; city-folk understand and can readily identify the heretic, hence he avoids cities. He prefers to visit hamlets and villages; to convert even the children who herd the geese in the fields. Previously, the heretics made their advances clothed in religious garbs, and they swore under oath to everything they said, which made it easy to recognize them.[31] But, Berthold says:

Nû wandelent sie ir leben und ir ketzerîe rehte als der mâne, der sich dâ wandelet in sô manige wîse. Alsô tragent nû die ketzer swert unde mezzer, langez hâr, langez gewant, unde swerent die eide nû. Sie haeten etewenne den tôt ê geliten, wan sie sprâchen, got der haete in eide verboten. . . . Sê, unsaeliger ketzer, hât dir ez got verboten, wie mac danne dîn meister iemer erlouben? . . . wie mohte dir der erlouben daz dir got verboten hât? Dâ sol er ie zwelf kristen ze ketzern machen: dâ mite sol er den eit haben gebüezet. Pfî . . . ketzer! ob man dich danne ê ûf einer hürde verbrennete, ê danne dû einigen ketzer gemachest! Nû seht, wie verdampt ir gloube und ir leben ist! (I 403, 37 ff.)

They who say that mortal sin is non-existent, are heretics. Berthold adds that anyone may fall into mortal sin.[32] Furthermore, the preacher accuses those of heresy who are of the opinion that hell might be good in some respects: that God will build them mansions in hell, which does not at all seem impossible to them.[33]

All persons who have become disloyal to the Christian faith are the worst murderers of souls in the whole world; they are the heretics who Berthold says are known as: *Manachêi, Patrîne, Pôver-*

---

[29] Cf. I 295, 32 f.; 242, 31.

[30] Cf. I 295, 33 ff. Here, then, Berthold challenges the heretic: " Pfî, her ketzer! war umbe stêt ir dâ vor mînen ougen? unde woltet ir guotiu dinc lêren, war umbe stêt ir zuo mir niht, als ir vor den einvaltigen liuten dâ sprechet in dem winkel? " (I 295, 30 ff.).

[31] Cf. I 403, 31 ff.; 30, 33 ff.

[32] Cf. II 66, 18 ff.   [33] Cf. II 227, 2 ff.

lewe, Runkeler, Sporer, Sîfrider, Arnolder,[34] *Ortlieber, Gazarî,* and *Ariâni.*[35] Of them, Berthold says they have one hundred fifty different heresies; some believing what others disbelieve.[36] And,

Swenne ir einer hât funden ein iteniuwe ketzerîe, unde swelhe der selbe ie nâch im hât brâht in die selben ketzerîe, diu ketzerîe heizet danne alse jener, der sie von êrste dâ vant. (I 402, 11 ff.)

Berthold classifies as untruth and heresy the belief of those who think they may not perform their marital privilege after having had the occasion to receive Extreme Unction. In God's name, they are assured they may continue as previously. Likewise, Berthold corrects others who are under the impression that they may no longer eat meat and sleep on sheets after reception of Extreme Unction.[37]

In passing, Berthold says he does not wish ever to speak of the *dalmut* because it contains so many *verfluochtiu ketzerîe.* Moreover, because it tells of such *boesiu dinc.*[38]

Lastly, Berthold outlines seven of the more common heresies, which he would like to have set into simple, understandable ballads for everyone to sing, so the people could recognize these heresies. This should be done to counteract the songs composed by heretics to spread heresy.[39] The first of the seven irreligious teachings, therefore:

. . . swer dâ sprichet, ez müge dehein êman bî sîner hûsfrouwen geligen âne houbetsünde. . . . Daz ander . . . swer dâ sprichet, ez müge dehein rihter nieman ertoeten âne houbetsünde. . . . Daz dritte . . . daz die sieben heilikeit unde der wîhebrunne niht kraft enhaben. . . . Daz vierde . . . daz ein priester, der selbe in houbetsünde ist, daz der nieman von sînen sünden enbinden müge. . . . Daz fünfte . . . man sülle der wârheit niht swern und ez sî houbetsünde swer der rehten wârheit swer. Daz sehste . . . der die schrift nie gelêret wart unde wil doch ûz der schrift reden, alsô daz er sprichet: 'ez sprichet sant Gregorius, sant Augustînus, sant Bernhart.'[40] . . . Daz sibende . . . swer zwêne röcke habe, der sulle durch got einen geben: swer des niht tuo sî ewiclîche verlorn. (I 406, 9 ff.)

[34] Cf. I 130, 24-31 *passim.* Cf. Keil, *op. cit.,* 190; for a more detailed discussion, cf. Michael, *op. cit.,* II 266-300.
[35] II 70, 20.   [37] Cf. I 304, 10-20 *passim.*
[36] Cf. I 402, 10 f.   [38] Cf. I 401, 35 ff.   [39] Cf. I 405, 38 ff.
[40] " Berthold dépend surtout de saint Augustin, de sant Grégoire, de

d. *Sacrilege and Simony*

Berthold offers comparatively meagre material for the sins in this category. In one instance, he blames monastic greed for the prevalence of these vices. The guilty are warned that if one farthing is found in their possession *ân urlâp dîner meisterschaft*, their souls shall be condemned. *Mali religiosi, mali laici,* which are the results of the doings of the *sihtige tiuvel.*[41]

... klôsterliute mit symonîe, die geistlîche gâbe koufent oder verkoufent, und alle die eigenschefte in klôstern hânt über ir meisterschefte willen . . . und alle die kirchen hânt und die niezen wellent und dâ bî lebent, als leien. Symonîe . . . sacrilêjer, bistû iendert hie? Hüete dich, der morder hât sîn axt gesliffen!   (II 69, 37 ff.)

Berthold states in another sermon that if only civil and ecclesiastical authorities would unite, think similarly, stand by and help each other, no one would dare perform the sacrilegious deeds and simony which take place so frequently in churches.[42]

Noblemen, too, are included in the preacher's reproaches. Formerly, Berthold says, they endowed monasteries and churches; and many noblemen were made Saints: *künic Constantinus, keiser Heinrich, künic Karle, der künic von Engelant sant Ôswalt, künic Stephân von Ungern, sant Wenzeslaus von Bêheim,* and *ein herzoge sant Mauricius.*[43] But now, many monasteries are impoverished and ruined;

... daz man küme ûf vier pfarren ein armez pfeffelîn vindet von iuwer symonîe unde von iuwer sacrilegje.   (I 450, 12 ff.)

There are, in the view of Theologians, four species of superstitions: 1. improper worship of the true God; 2. idolatry; 3. divination; 4. vain observances, which include magic and occult arts. Their origin is subjective: ignorance of natural causes which leads to the belief that certain striking phenomena express the will of some invisible overruling power, and the objects in which such phenomena appear are forthwith deified. Conversely, many superstitious practices are due to an exaggerated notion or a false

saint Bernard et d'Alexandre de Halès, il est avant tout auteur moral et ascétique." *Dictionnaire de Spiritualité Ascétique et Mystique* (Paris, 1937), 1533.
[41] Cf. I 394, 19 ff.   [42] Cf. I 363, 35 ff.   [43] Cf. I 449, 37 ff.

interpretation of natural events, so that effects are sought which are beyond the efficiency of physical causes.

Although, in the middle of the thirteenth century, superstition had been eliminated to some extent by the preaching of Christianity, the tendency to which the cause gave rise was so deep-rooted that many of the ancient practices survived and, apparently according to Berthold, these practices were still applied extensively. It was only by degrees, through the legislation of the Church and the advance of scientific knowledge, that the earlier forms of superstition were eradicated. In addition to the employment of the Host, toads, wild apples, charms, etc., which Berthold sermonizes against, superstition of any description is a transgression of the First Commandment; it is also against the positive law of the Church, and against the natural law inasmuch as it runs counter to the dictates of reason in the matter of man's relation to God.[44]

The sin of superstition is also committed by giving divine honor to false gods. Material idolatry is a grave sin, for it is directly against the obligation of making eternal profession of the faith, and contains the grave malice of a lie in matters of religion. Formal idolatry is perfect or imperfect. The former consists in honoring a creature as God, falsely thinking it to be God. The latter knowingly honors a creature as God, without any excuse of ignorance, out of hatred towards Him, or wishing to obtain something thereby. This form is more grievous on account of the greater knowledge and malice.[45] Concerning the scarcity of material in Berthold's sermons on idolatry, it may be said that Berthold did not find it necessary to elaborate upon an evil, pagan practice which, by his time, had been obliterated in Christian countries.

St. Thomas (IIa IIae q. 11, a. 1) defines heresy: "a species of infidelity in men who, having professed the faith of Christ, corrupt its dogmas." There are two ways of deviating from Christianity: the one by refusing to believe in Christ Himself, which is the way of infidelity common to Pagans and Jews; the other by restricting

[44] Cf. *Catholic Encyclopedia*, XIV, 339 f., St. Thomas Aquinas, IIa IIae q. 42, a. 1; q. 44, a. 4.

[45] Cf. T. Slater, S. J., *A Manual of Moral Theology* (New York, Chicago, 1908), I 216 f.

belief to certain points of Christ's doctrine selected and fashioned at pleasure, which is the way of heretics.

Heresy in the Middle Ages differed from ancient heresy mainly in that its aim and interest was ecclesiastical and practical rather than doctrinal, though doctrinal it was. That is to say, it was the protest of individualism against an established order.[46]

Heresy has always been punished by the Church as a crime which attacks the foundations and the very *raison d'être* of her existence. In order to incur the penalties inflicted on heresy, the sin must be both formal and external, for the Church in her external forum does not take cognizance of the sins of thought. The external act must be such as of its own nature, or from custom, or from the special circumstances, is held sufficient to manifest an heretical mind.[47]

Sacrilege is the irreverent treatment of sacred persons, places, and things. The irreverence consists in doing something which is especially repugnant to the sanctity of the object in respect of its sacred character. A person, place or thing becomes sacred by being dedicated to the service of God by public authority, for it does not seem possible that the dedication of an object to God by private authority should be able to lay an obligation on others to treat it with the reverence due to sacred things. The irreverence shown to sacred things redounds to the dishonor of God, to whose service they are dedicated.

Simony is a studious endeavor to buy or sell for a temporal advantage, something which is spiritual, or which is annexed to what is spiritual. Simony may also be mental: when no contract is entered into between the parties. Simony, like sacrilege, is a grave sin, and if it is against the divine law it is always mortal. If the simony be merely against ecclesiastical law it is also of itself a mortal sin, but inasmuch as it is constituted by ecclesiastical prohibition and a sin of disobedience is only venial when the matter is trivial, there may consequently be venial sins of that simony which is merely of ecclesiastical law.[48] But Berthold does not draw the distinction in his treatment of simony; to him, this vice is " one

[46] Cf. G. Cross, *Encyclopedia of Religion and Ethics*, VI, 618; also C. U. Hahn, *Geschichte der Ketzer im Mittelalter* (Stuttgart, 1845).
[47] Cf. Slater, *op. cit.*, 176.   [48] Cf. *ibid.*, 226 ff., 231 ff.

of the worst in the world," and all his censures are directed to
monks, and noblemen.

B. THE SECOND COMMANDMENT

Part I

Dû solt dînes gotes namen niht unnützelîchen nennen. Berthold
occupies himself immediately with the first division: *daz dû weder
durch liebe noch durch leide noch durch miete noch durch dehein
dinc meineide swern solt noch umbe sus der wârheit niht swern
solt.*

a. Oaths

Berthold complains that in the taking of an unnecessary oath,
regardless of its intrinsic truth, one breaks the second commandment. To further his explanation, Berthold says:

Man swert der wârheit âne sünde wol, diu nütze unde reht ist unde des
man niht geraten mac. . . . Man sol halt eide swern, die dâ wâr sint unde
reht sint und êrbaere an swern sint unde danne nütze sint. . . .

The attitude of heretics toward oaths is distorted, since they maintain *man sülle der wârheit niht swern.* Berthold classifies this as a
lie, and says that St. John wrote in the Apocalypse that an angel
swore; and Holy Scripture even tells that God Himself swore and
has sworn.

He bitterly attacks the individual who would take an oath for
one of his friends; and even if it were for his own brother, he
should rather have him hacked into a thousand pieces. Otherwise
he will contaminate the very land on which he lives, and he re-
nounces thereby all help of God, saints, and the Blessed Mother.[49]
Priests are commanded to impose heavy, and strict penances on
such persons.[50]

The speaker introduces a setting which embraces several classes
of offenders:

Pfî, ir krâmer unde pfragener und ir schuochsiuter und ir andern alle, die
ze markte stênt mit ir veilen koufe, wie ofte unde wie dicke ir daz ander
gebot zerbrechet!

[49] Cf. I 27, 17 ff.   [50] Cf. I 116, 2 ff.

Berthold reproves these merchants for the sheer indifference and
unconstraint with which they take superfluous oaths:

Wann daz ir eins pfenninges wert verkoufet daz ir veile habet, sô habet ir
vil lîhte vier eide gesworn. . . . Unde kumet sîn in eine gewonheit, daz ir
einen eit umb einigen holzapfel swert oder gar umbe sus.

He further cautions the whole world against foreswearers, for
God's sake, since there are thousands who have become so accus-
tomed to swearing, that they can scarcely speak unless

. . . sie enswern bî gote unde bî sîner reinen muoter unde bî allen sînen
heiligen dar zuo.

b. Vows

Vows, as such, are briefly discussed in connection with Marriage
and Baptism. By the very act of adultery, Berthold says, the
guilty have perjured themselves, for they have broken the oath of
loyalty and truth. Although married women *swernt niht eide*, they
are bound to the marriage vow just as much as men; and the married woman must never say: ' *ich geswuor im nie deheine triuwe
ze leisten: ich bin wol ledic.*' To this Berthold adds:

Nû sich, êbrecher und êbrecherin. . . . Nû bist dû triuwelôs an dîner ê, nû
bist dû meineidic dîner gelübede, nû hâst dû dîn selbes heilikeit gevelschet
unde zerbrochen als vil sô ez an dir was.[51]

Addressing innocent persons, Berthold makes a reference to bap-
tismal vows:

haltet iuch in der gelübede, die ir dem almehtigen got entheizen habet in
dem heiligen toufe, als der guote sante Niclaus . . . Uolrîch . . . Kathe-
rînâ . . . und der andern ein michel teil.   (I 68, 19 ff.)

Part II of Second Commandment

The subdivision of the commandment under discussion is: *daz
dû got niht schelten solt und im niht fluochen solt.*

c. Blasphemy

By breaking this mandate, one alienates himself from God. In
the opinion of Berthold, blasphemy is such a great sin that in one

[51] Cf. I 279, 13-29, *passim.*

night an angel of God slew one hundred eighty thousand persons because of one who had blasphemed Him.[52*] Berthold addresses himself in this instance directly and especially to gamblers and dice players, and inquires of them:

Wie gevellet iu daz, ir spiler und ir toppeler, die got scheltent, sô ez niht nâch ir willen vellet? [53*]

Were it not for God's goodness and mercy, the earth would open and swallow the blasphemer on the very spot where he blasphemed God and His dear Mother. For the sake of Almighty God, then, the good people are enjoined not to allow a blasphemy on God or His holy Mother to enter their hearts or to cross their lips. Blasphemers ought to be brought before the civil and ecclesiastical tribunals, so that they may receive two-fold judgment. Berthold describes the procedure which should characterize the two courts:

Geistlîche rihter sullen sie villen und schern vor der kirchen gewalt, unde sol im ofte buoze geben dar nâch, wan diu schulde ist vor der kirchen menie. Unde der werltlîche rihter sol im hût unde hâr abe heizen slahen, gebunden an einer siule, oder mit pfenningen büezen.[54*]

Berthold considered this sin such an extraordinary one that he demanded torture as a punishment.

Blasphemy is a powerful ally of the devil which leads thousands of souls to serve him because

er ist alse gar selbherre, daz er den menschen machet, daz er sîn selbes niht bekennet, und an im erblendet alle die bescheidenheit, der im nôt unde durft waere an sîner sele.   (I 531, 20 ff.)

Furthermore, blasphemers become easily calloused in mind and heart; they wage war, *beide heimlîche in ir muote und ouch offenlîche*, against Holy Scripture. And from blasphemy arises most of the disloyalty and heresy which transform the victim into a proud, selfish, selfwilled personality (*selbherren gemüete*), and engenders a strong, defiant will (*selbherren willen*). The guilty, Berthold says, regard the Ten Commandments as troublesome; they

---

[52] Cf. I 83, 39 ff.

[53] Cf. I 231, 13 ff. The delinquents are further warned that, even if they do not blaspheme God, by the very act of gambling they commit a capital sin. Cf. I 267, 4 ff.

[54] Cf. I 362-363 *passim*.

war against them and they are inclined to believe that God will never become so angry that He would condemn a soul for sinning against such trifles. They gradually lull their consciences to sleep, and they lead others away from the Word of God.

Berthold enjoins the people to combat blasphemy with the virtue of Christian wisdom (*diu guote erkantnisse*). As on several other instances, he compares virtues to virgins, and he likens this last one as well to a virgin. Whoever loves this virgin, values his soul and God, and he appreciates everything with which he may gain God's grace. Moreover, continues the preacher, he values God's Word and teaching: the Word of God is God Himself, and whosoever scorns His Word, scorns Him.[55]

d. Cursing and Swearing

Berthold warns parents of the devil's constant endeavor to ensnare children immediately after they have been baptized. As soon as they have learned to walk and to talk, the devil busies himself with counseling and inducing children to learn bad words, and speak abusive words, and to blaspheme and to curse. The preacher laments that parents are unmoved by this; on the contrary, he maintains, they seem to find it amusing and a sign of precociousness in their offspring.[56]

Those who make it a practice to curse domestic animals commit sin.[57] It is a greater sin, however, to curse a fellow-Christian,[58] for it is said in the Holy Gospel:

' swer zuo dem andern alsô sprichet in rehtem ernste: dû affe, der ist des schuldic, daz er iemer brinnen muoz.'

To curse Our Blessed Mother is a still greater sin; and the most horrible sin is to curse Almighty God.[59]

Lastly, the people are warned against the usage of any evil word, because this commandment shall be strictly enforced; and Berthold says of himself:

Jâ wolte ich niht einem hunde oder einer katzen fluochen . . . sô dû fluochest aller der werlte herre.

---

[55] Cf. I 531-533 *passim*.

[56] Cf. I 33, 10 ff.

[57] Cf. I 117, 18 f.

[58] Cf. *ibid.*, 17; 267, 21.

[59] Cf. I 117, 21 ff.

According to the teaching of Christian theologians, there cannot be an oath strictly so-called unless there be the intention of swearing and a suitable form of words be used which express that intention. Those who use colloquialisms usually have no intention of taking an oath, nor do the words signify an intention of calling upon God to witness the truth of what is said. However, if there be an intention to take an oath, this will be sufficient to make it binding in conscience whatever the form of words may be, so that perjury will be committed if what is asserted is not true. If the form of words is suitable for an oath, the intention to swear is presumed. If the requisite conditions be fulfilled oaths are lawful, and indeed they are an act of divine worship, for they are an acknowledgment of the omniscience and veracity of God, as well as a public profession of belief in Him.

Berthold evidences great concern for oaths sworn by people, but it may be said that he is confusing profane language with something of a graver nature. Here he is undoubtedly occupied with the thought of exhorting his auditors against common swearing and abuse of God's name.

A vow is a deliberate promise made to God to do or to omit some act, the performance or the omission of which is possible, and more perfect than the opposite. Such an act binds the conscience. The act must be perfectly human, performed with full knowledge, and complete use of reason. If the matter of the vow be impossible, the promise does not bind; it must be something which is physically and morally possible.

The annulment of a vow may be direct or indirect. By direct annulment the obligation of a vow is altogether removed by one who has authority over the will of the person who took the vow. By indirect annulment the obligation is suspended by one who has the authority over the matter of the vow. A husband can directly annul the vows of his wife taken after marriage, and indirectly those taken previously. A wife can annul the vows of husband only indirectly, as far as they prejudice her rights.[60]

Blasphemy is direct when the dishonor of God is intended; if

---

[60] Cf. St. Alphonsus M. Liguori, *Instructions on the Commandments and Sacraments*, trans. by a Catholic Clergyman (Boston, no date), 88 f., also Slater, *op. cit.*, 246 ff.

the dishonor of God is not intended in itself but it is foreseen that it will be the consequence of one's words or actions, it is indirect.[61] Distinction is made, of course, from expressions uttered which simply proceed from impatience, but are not previously injurious to a saint or holy thing. Berthold does not honor the distinction which should be made.

In his treatment of the second commandment, another great moralist, St. Alphonsus, employs a term which is almost identical with one Berthold uses: " I wonder that, at every blasphemy, the earth does not open under the feet of the man who utters it." [62]

C. THE THIRD COMMANDMENT

Part I

The third *helbelinc* is the third commandment: *dû solt dînen ruowetac heilic machen.* Of the two divisions, the first is: *dû solt an dem ruowetac niht wirken vor smâcheit unde vor unwirde als die ketzer, die an dem suntage gerner wirkent danne an dem mântage.*

a. *Prohibition to Work on Sunday*

Work of any kind which cannot be deferred until another day, may be performed on Sunday. However, throughout the whole world, Sundays, and all days *die man iu bî dem banne gebiutet ze vîren,* should be observed as days of complete rest. In an ironic tone, Berthold speaks of a common violation of the third precept: the populace goes about on holy Sundays and on feasts of the Apostles, in wagons and carts, with horses and mules, into the fields, into the country, to the markets, to towns, and to villages, instead of remaining at home to rest. Berthold speaks also of masters who do their servants injustice by requiring too much of them on days of rest.

Dû kneht, dir tuot dîn herre unrehte, der dich an dem ruowetage deheiner arbeit noetet für baz danne daz dû im sîn vihe ûz und în trîbest an die weide oder ez im dâ heime etzest unde trenkest. . . . Und dû dierne, dîn meister tuot dir unrehte oder dîn herre oder dî frouwe, swenne sie dich

---

[61] Cf. Slater, *op. cit.*, 238.
[62] Cf. St. Alphonsus, *op. cit.*, 77, 81.

ihtes iht heizent wirken an dem ruowetage danne ein ezzen machen unde
diu kint besehen oder ein vihe; des mac man niht gerâten.

He sometimes dramatically speaks directly to dumb animals of the
injustice of their masters towards them; and he flays their owners
in no uncertain terms when they make them violate the days of
rest.
Later, Berthold makes the announcement:

Ir sult ouch dar umbe niht tanzen an dem ruowetage oder spîln oder
toppeln, daz ir niht ze tuonne habet;

and he acknowledges the objections raised by some of the congregation against the above injunction. They accuse him of making *den
wec gar enge*. And so to the inquiry:

sê, we suln wir danne tuon daz wir den tac vertrîben?

Berthold replies that the day should be spent according to the
decree of God. Sunday should be made holy: one should do nothing but holy deeds—assist at Mass, call fervently upon God for
His blessings, pray devoutly and spend a part of the day in Church,
in good behavior. Thereafter, the people should return to their
homes, eat, then sleep for a short time. Berthold gives additional
suggestions as to how the day's activities may be concluded with
propriety:

. . . sô sult ir danne aber zer kirchen gên oder dâ heimen iuwer gebet
getriuwelîche sprechen oder . . . sult ir . . . vertrîben mit . . . almuosen-
geben . . . mit venien, ze predigen gên . . . unde swâ ir aplâz und ander
gnâde vindet. Unde sult zuo den siechen gên . . . ir sult ouch gên, dâ
gevangene liute ligent, unde sult die troesten.

The prohibition of dancing on Sundays and holidays is a dis-
appointment to many of his hearers. They are impudent in their
protest:

Bruoder Berhtolt rede dû wellest! wir mügen ungetanzet niht sîn.

As a countercharge, he speaks the words of St. Augustine: " *ez ist
bezzer daz man an dem vîgertage z'acker gê danne man tanze.*"
Dancing on Sunday he considers a mortal sin. There is, however,
provided the one exception: namely, that a person may dance at a
wedding, on Sunday, without being guilty of a *mortal* sin. However, he adds:

Dû maht ouch alsô tanzen, daz dû *toetlîche* sünde tuost. Swer an dem
suntage z'acker gêt, der tuot toetlîche sünde. Der tanzet, der tuot daz
selbe. Der ackerganc ist aber nütze: sô ist daz tanzen nieman nütze.

The preacher, furthermore, is determined regarding a breach of
this divine commandment, adding that if one should dance, conduct himself boisterously, play dice, indulge in unchaste deeds,
commit perjury, steal, or be guilty of any other sin on Monday
and Tuesday, he causes Our Lord great pain. But to commit these
sins on Sunday causes Him still greater pain; the sin is all the
more heinous if the Sunday happens also to be a major feast day,
for instance Easter or Pentecost; for the holier the time, the
greater pain one causes God.[63]

Berthold shows concern, moreover, for those individuals who
spend Sundays working in the fields. Such a practice of vice, he
warns, will gain them nothing. Their hoped-for gain will vanish
either through divine intervention, or through temporal bereave-
ment. The unjust profits will not endure: they will be lost either
through theft, fire, or hail; or the one guilty of breaking the
Sabbath will languish in sickness or affliction until he is bereft of
the goods produced during forbidden times. Berthold, ironically
scornful, tells the people to continue working on Sundays like the
beast of burden, or as the devil himself who never rests. In a
similar vein he says:

Sê! nû sihst dû wol, daz ein stinkender jüde, der die liute an bokezet,
sînen vîgertac baz êret danne dû. Pfî! des möhtest dû kristener dich wol
schamen, daz dû got niht alse wol getrûwest als der stinkende jüde, ob dû
den vîgertac in sînem lobe vertribest, als er dir geboten hât daz er dich
des ergetzete.

Divine Providence never fails to replenish the needs of those who
obey its decrees; yet there are many who are so totally disaffected
by its gifts that they grumble and beg for greater things. Some
complain directly to God:

owê, herre, wie hâst dû mich sô gar unsaelic erschaffen, daz dû dem sô vil
gibest unde mir sô wênic.

To correct this delusion, Berthold ridicules their despondency. He
assures them that no matter how vociferously they growl for the

[63] Cf. I 446, 11 ff.

excessive luxuries of this world, God, in His wisdom, will allot to
them as He sees fit. The people are assured that God's gifts are
beyond measure,

wolte er dirz geben. Ich wil dir sagen, waz er hât, ob er dir geben wolte
. . . bereites guotes ûf ertrîche: âne daz er von sînen götlîchen genâden
allez ze geben hât, sô hât er grôze starke guldîne berge in Indiâ.

However, God has a purpose in not giving even a little of this to
everybody because possession may lead to false pride and a feeling
of Lordship:

Dû woltest gerne ein herre sîn, unde muost den acker bûwen. Sô wolte der
gerne ein grâve sîn, der muoz ein schuochsûter sîn. Daz selbe spriche ich
zuo allen arbeitern. Haete uns got alle ze herren gemachet, sô waere diu
werlt unverrihtet unde würde ouch selten wol unde rehte stênde in dem
lande.

Part II of the Third Commandment

The remaining part of the third commandment is: *daz dînes
herzen ruowe an deheiner kreâtûre sol sîn danne an got alleine, der
alliu dinc beschaffen hât.*

The development of this section evidences the preacher's charac-
teristic, but pardonable tendency towards discursiveness and repeti-
tion. In this second division of the third commandment are found
discussions of capital sins, and two virtues: love of God, and love of
neighbor. This method peculiar to himself, he employs for the
sake of good balance.

Vehemently and at great length, Berthold, in discussing the third
commandment again, exposes and condemns the prevalence and
profligacy of greed, since greed never rests, not even on Sunday.
In the sense of desire for power, greed is more wicked than avarice.
Even the poor are not safe from the persecutions of the avaricious.
Through taking exhorbitant interests, through their preëmptions,
their usury, their presumptuous manipulation of God's own time,
the greedy and avaricious are willing tools of the devil. And while
the world is at rest, the *verdamptiu arbeit* of the avaricious
progresses: their financial ploughs operate uninterruptedly day and
night, winter and summer, week-day and Sunday, in good and bad
weather; and in many other ways so that even the devil damns
them by their own sins. Accordingly, then, Berthold says to them:

. . . wan in aller der werlte ist niendert sünder sô arger, er gerouwe etewie vil wîle mit sînen sünden, wan dû.

Subsequently, Berthold interpolates five other auxiliary vices that sentence the avaricious to perdition:

Sô ist dîn ander verdampnisse, daz dû dîner sünden niemer sat wirdest, daz dich ir niemer genüeget. Etewenne wirt einer luoders, unde spiles sat, einer unkiusche, einer zornes, einer tanzes. Daz ist ouch dîn dritte verdampnisse und ist ouch diu wirste, daz dû aller wârer riuwe einige niht enhâst. Daz vierde ist, daz ir selten iemer dekeiner bekêret wirt, die dîne genôzen sint. Dehein sünder gelîchet sich dem tiuvel sô gar, sô der gîtige unde der ketzer, der lange in ketzerîe ist gewesen: der hât ouch dekeinen muot, daz er sich iemer bekêren welle. Sô ist daz diu fünfte verdampnisse, daz dû manic hundert sêle mit dir zer helle bringest.

Here the preacher manifestly vociferates against the satanic operations of the avaricious:

Ir mörder, ir schâcher, ir verdampnet iuwer eines sêle; der sünder ist gar vil, die niuwer ir einiges sêle verdamnent. Sô verdampnest dû alle, die daz unrehte guot wizzentlîche nâch dir erbent. Dû ertoetest dîne sêle niht alleine: dû ertoetest alle die, die ez nâch dir erbent wizzentlîche, als ich iezuo sprach.

The unjust acquisition of property, whether through inheritance or otherwise, is palpably iniquitous. Berthold tells those who are guilty in this respect, namely, those heirs who are conscious of the fact that the goods are not rightfully theirs, and who nevertheless do not make restitution, shall be cast into the depths of hell. Innocent people are even cautioned that, for the sake of Almighty God, their children should not be given in marriage to children who have inherited ill-gotten goods, because they are thus sold to eternal death.

Berthold warns persons guilty of avarice that the third is a serious commandment for them, and he continues to say:

Swie maniger marke wert dû habest, er waere dir vil nützer unde bezzer, swenne dîn sêle von dînem lîbe scheiden muoz, danne alle die kelre vol wînes unde danne alle dîne stedel vol kornes und alle dîne schrîne volle schatzes. Ich spriche mêr: er waere dir halt nützer danne alle guldîne berge.

Whoever keeps this third commandment has, ipso facto, adhered to all the others. To him, the sins of pride, envy, hatred, anger, etc., and others, which draw him away from God, are repulsive and so, again for balance, Berthold dwells upon another vice. Acrimonious reproaches are hurled at the drinker, and drinking, of course, was most popular on Sundays:

> . . . iuwer ein michel teil iu ist der helbelinc eht gar tiure, waz dîn herze brinnet ze allen zîten nâch wîne: des morgens dâ zer kirchen, die niht erbîten mügent, unz man die messe gar ûz gesinget, er engê hin ze dem wîne. Ist aber daz er blîbet unze man den segen gît, sô wirt im ofte unde dicke sô gâch, daz er niemer gar volle gestêt unze man den segen gar volle getuot, wan daz im der segen hinden an den nak wirt. Pfî! dû möhtest in doch under diu ougen enpfâhen! jâ geizzest dû sîn dannoch genuoc dar allen den tac.

To amplify his absolute repugnance towards drinkers, Berthold asserts that their contentment in their sodden ways strikes an indistinguishable balance with dancing and unchastity.

Prior to his final comments on the third commandment, Berthold includes several features concerning the zeal one should evince in his love of God. To clarify and to give reasons why everyone should love God above all else, he asks rhetorically: if you had your own servants who rightfully had to serve you, and who had received from you everything they needed, and had been saved by you from death, you would certainly expect their service and love for you to strengthen proportionately. Since man was created to serve God for His benefit, we should offer Him praise and honor, and thank Him for His loyalty and love. One is to love his neighbor and property only in so far as this does not break God's Commandment, lest he lose thereby His love and affection. The people should remember that:

> Got versuochet dich niht als Abrahâmen, daz dû dîn kint toetest. Dû soltest ez aber ê lâzen toeten danne dû gotes hulde verlürest. Owê, lieber got! waz werlte umbe disen helbelinc wirt verlorn unde verdampt, daz sie diz gebot niht haltent!

Before Berthold proceeds to the fourth commandment, he departs from his regular arrangement of presentation, and incorporates several contributory remarks in connection with the third ordinance. The assemblage is informed that the first three commandments are in relation to God, and the following seven pertain to one's fellow-man. Nevertheless, if an individual transgress any one of the injunctions, his soul is lost. The expressions which follow, uttered by some members of the congregation, are in some degree illustrative of the medieval religious naïveté:

Owê, bruoder Berhtolt, wie sullen wir daz allez behalten, daz daz dû uns vor seist? Möhtest dû uns einen wec vinden zem himelrîche, der uns senfter unde ringer waere! unde haeten wir halt minner freuden in dem himel: swâ wir in einem winkel waeren oder hinder der türe, dâ diuhtez mich gar unde gar guot.

In answer to this exhibition of simplicity and ignorance of the fundamentals of religion, Berthold exclaims:

Nû in gotes namen! sô lange und ir niht groezer freuden in den hôhen koeren begert, sô geschaehe mir aber niemer leider, ob ich iu in den nider- sten kôr braehte unde zuo dem nidersten lône dâ ze himele. . . . Diu zehen gebot sint der rehte wec zem himelrîche . . . sô mac nieman dar komen âne diu zehen gebot.

The congregation is told that every Christian ought to be thoroughly familiar with the Divine Orders, and that in days gone by, the people even made and hung up written mementoes in order to be less inclined to do that which would be contrary to God's rules; and that they bound thorns to their feet so they would be reminded of the commandments. So, for God's sake, the priests must preach all the more concerning the Ten Commandments.[64] Finally, Berthold interjects supplemental counsel: when one is confronted with an occasion of sin, he must immediately think of the Sacred Precepts in order to preserve himself from eternal death; he must not rationalize:

---

[64] R. Cruel, *Geschichte d. d. Predigt im Mittelalter*, 610, proves that Luther and Matthesius were in error when they complained that the Ten Commandments were never heard of, or preached about. Cruel uses Berthold and decisions of various synods as counter attacks to point out the falsity of their statements. The Ten Commandments must have been frequently preached; and instruction on them was often given. P. Göbl, *Geschichte der Katechese im Abendlande vom Verfalle des Katechumenats bis zum Ende des Mittelalters* (Kempten, 1880), 180, says that the thirteenth century demanded instruction in the Ten Commandments. Furthermore, he says that the Decalogue is found in the old " Pönitential- bücher," in Old German " Beichtdenkmäler " (p. 176) and continued on down through the centuries. Instruction on the Decalogue was included in the spiritual life for all, not only the young, in the decisions of synods which Göbl traces from 1340 to 1548 (169 ff.).

. . . briche ich daz gebot, daz mac ich noch gar wol gebüezen. Geloube mir, dû bist vaste betrogen . . . sô waere diu sünde doch hundertstunt bezzer ze mîden danne ze büezen.

It is noteworthy that Berthold only once, and in that instance very casually, mentions the *obligation* of assisting at Mass on Sundays. Such an obligation is imposed by the third precept. The precept of sanctifying the Sunday, inasmuch as it commands to honor God by some worship at some part of our life, according to St. Thomas, and the generality of theologians, belongs to the moral part of the law; so that all are bound by a natural obligation to observe it. " Quantum ad hoc quod homo deputet aliquod tempus vitae suae ad vacandum divinis." (St. Thomas IIa IIae q. 122 a. 4. ad. 1 et 4.)

Concerning the obligation of abstaining from servile works, it is necessary in Christian doctrine to distinguish three kinds of works—servile, liberal, and common. Servile works are, as St. Thomas teaches (3 sent. dist. 37, q. 2, a. 5 ad. 7) in the mystic sense, sins, but literally, they are the works which are performed only by servants. They are also called corporal works. Liberal works, or occupations, which are called works of the mind, are those performed by men in a liberal condition of life. These are permitted on holy days, even though performed for gain. Common works are those which are performed by servants and by men in a liberal condition of life.[65] In these matters, if the precept cannot be observed without serious inconvenience, it ceases to bind. Work in the direct service of religion, or necessary works of charity are not forbidden. Necessary occupations around the house may be attended to on Sundays.

---

[65] Cf. St. Alphonsus, *op. cit.*, 91 f., 93 f.

CHAPTER III

SINS AGAINST THE LAST SEVEN COMMANDMENTS

The last seven commandments are regarded by Berthold himself, and other theologians as a unit apart from the first three that pertain to man's duties to God alone. The remaining seven detail the obligations of a single command: Love thy neighbor as theyself. " Owe no man anything but to love one another. For he that loveth his neighbor hath fulfilled the law. For *Thou shalt not commit adultery: Thou shalt not kill: Thou shalt not steal: Thou shalt not bear false witness: Thou shalt not covet:* and if there be any other commandment, it is comprised in this word, THOU SHALT LOVE THY NEIGHBOR AS THYSELF. . . . Love is the fulfilling of the law." (Romans 13/ 8-10.)

The Fourth Commandment

Part I

Dû solt êren vater unde muoter, die dich an die werlt brâhten is the first section of the fourth commandment *dû solt êren dînen vater unde dîne muoter daz dû lancleben habest.*

a. Obligation of Honoring Parents

In his utterances on the fourth commandment Berthold unveils another most prevalent sin of the times, namely, the transgressions against parents. Parents must be held in honor, that is, they must not be scorned or neglected even though they be poor, ill, deformed, unattractive, and weak, he says. They may have come to such a state through filial dereliction; therefore children ought not to spurn their parents or be ashamed of father or mother, lest they be denied entrance into God's Kingdom. Mockery of parents is one of the greatest evils prevalent in the world. Berthold commands ingrates who reprove and strike parents: *vil wunderlîchen balde in starke buoze oder an den grunt der helle!* All who dishonor father and mother merit divers strictures:

7

Daz eine, daz er dâ mite daz himelrîche hât verworht.   Daz ander, er hât sîn erbe dâ mite verworht.   Daz dritte, er hât sîn lancleben verworht.   Daz vierde, er hât einen unrehten tôt mite verdienet.

For the sake of Almighty God, then, people should be ever mindful of the curse that will be upon them if they do not honor their parents.   Jews and heathens pay honor to their superiors more than a large number of Christians do, thus the latter are warned to protect themselves against the horrible curse they may have to hear on Judgment Day.[1]

Part II of Fourth Commandment

The preacher continues his discussion of the commandment with the second division: *dû solt dînen geistlîchen vater êren; daz sint die priester, wan die hât got selbe gewirdiget unde geêret über alle menschen.*

b. Obligation of Honoring Clerics

Berthold expands this order briefly.   He busies himself here chiefly with the respect which persons should give to the sacerdotal dignity.   Priests are to be honored by word and deed, *unde gein in ûf stên, swâ man sie siht.*   Observe, for instance:

Und waere ein dinc, daz mîn frouwe sante Marîâ ûf erden waere mit allen gotes heiligen unde saezen dâ schône bî einander unde gienge ein priester zuo in: sie solten gegen im ûf stên, wan er tuot daz sie alle samt niht getuon mügent.[2*]

Because of the sublime dignity of the priesthood, implying that the priest is God's representative on earth,[3*] the whole world, then, is urged to tender priests reverential respect; everyone, therefore, should be on guard lest he offend God through disrespect to His chosen instruments of mercy.

. . . daz man in (priest) iht leides tuo.[4*]   Sie sint iu gar ze starke an iu ze rechin mit übeln dingen.

The discussion concludes with this injunction:

[1] Cf. II 216, 18-26 *passim.*   [2] Cf. I 164, 3 ff.
[3] Cf. I 301, 26 ff.; 452, 3 ff.   The powers of the Holy Priesthood are discussed I 305, 5 ff.; II 91, 29 ff.
[4] Cf. I 452, 11 ff.

Ir sult ouch êren iuwern geistlîchen muoter, daz ist diu heilige kristenheit,
daz dû dînen ebenkristen êrest . . . daz wir kristenliute alle einander ge-
brüeder sîn in gote, als wir alle tage dâ sprechen in dem pater noster.

This commandment explicitly regards the obligations of children
towards parents; implicitly, also, the obligations of all inferiors
towards their superiors, and the correlative obligations of superiors
towards their inferiors. Children are bound to love, reverence, and
obey their parents: to love them because of the natural union
between parent and child, and by reason of the benefits received;
to reverence them, because of a parent's dignity and authority, the
dignity of coöperation in creation, the authority in the natural
unit of society, which is the family; to obey them, because the
parent has a right and duty to educate the child physically, morally,
religiously, and intellectually. Love and reverence are absolute and
perpetual obligations; obedience is conditional and temporary.[5]

Berthold does not mention the duties of parents, and the duties
of other states in life, which are ordinarily discussed under this
precept.

The Fifth Commandment

Part I

The fifth commandment, *dû solt nieman toeten*, has the first part
*dû solt nieman toeten mit dîn selbes hant; dû solt ouch nieman
heizen toeten. Wan den haetest ouch ertoetet, unde dem dû wol
gehelfen möhtest unde des niht entuost.*

a. Murder

Here again, the manner in which Berthold elaborates is unex-
pected. He opens his discussion by informing the people that if
one were to disobey the command *gip dem hungerigen z'ezzen*, and
the hungry one should die, the guilt would lie on the one able
to feed the needy. The avaricious are again reproached, and in no
uncertain terms the preacher reproves them for their selfish,
unchristian ways:

[5] Cf. H. Davis, S. J., *Moral and Pastoral Theology*, I 69. Cf. St. Thomas
Aquinas, IIa IIae q. 101.

Pfî! gîtiger, an wie manigem bistû schuldic? Wan dû laezest ê erfûlen
daz edel korn, ê daz dû ez umbe rehten kouf gaebest: ich wil geswîgen
umbe sus.   Dû wirdest . . . schuldic . . . die dû alle von hunger laezest
sterben.   Dû stêst eht allenthalben an dem blate.   Daz ist ouch dîner
verdampnisse einiu. . . .

A violation of the fifth commandment is, in the spirit of the
times, one of the worst crimes known to mankind; otherwise it
would not be one of the four sins that cry to heaven for vengeance.[6]
The preacher excoriates murder, and presents exhortations against
this offense: no one must desire the death of another by counsel,
connivance, or coöperation.   Berthold explains that even though
one does not commit murder directly, such a one is just as guilty if
he hires or even desires another to commit the murder.   Upon
these " manslaughterers " whom Berthold calls also *Kâins genôze*,[7]*
he imposes: *vil wunderlîchen balde in starke buoze, morder gotes
unde der werlte unde dîner armen sêle!*   And after the speaker
declares that he believes many *bluottrinker* [8]* to be his audience,
he bitterly asks whether the world has become wanting in water,
beer, mead, and wine, that they should see fit to spill human blood;
and he further interrogates whether they cannot be filled with
all the goats and oxen the world has, that they must devour human
flesh.[9]* Murderers are reminded that the blood of their victims
will accuse the guilty ones forever before heaven—it is one of the
four sins that are never silent before God.[10]   Discussing murder
at greater length, Berthold says:

Der wirt als vil bî dem ende der werlt, daz reht ein bluot in daz ander
fliuzet, und als vil wirt der selben sünde, daz sô grôz urliuge unde strît
wirt habende sich, daz sie sich sô sêre under einander slahent, daz ir beider
bluot under einander fliuzet.   (I 91, 31 ff.)

Then he informs the people that wars and bloodshed had already
been started,

dô der von Ungern unde von Bêheim dâ striten, daz manic man den
lîp verlôs.   Unde der künic von Frankrîche, der ouch einen grôzen strît
jensît mers tet; unde der grâve Pêter von Savoi unde grâve Rudolf von
Habichesburc, unde grâve Hermann von Hennenberc unde der bischof von
Wirzeburc, unde der künic Primze mit tiutschen liuten.   (I 91, 36 ff.)

[6] Cf. I 91, 26 ff.   [8] Cf. I 92, 7 ff.
[7] Cf. I 70, 23 ff.   [9] Cf. I 70, 26 ff.   [10] Cf. I 71, 14 ff.

All of these events took place in short time; and besides, many other murders were committed over a single word, or for a farthing of wine, or beer, or over ten apples, or pears.[11]

Berthold shows particular concern for persons who are given to extreme anger; for this, too, is the cause for many a murder. He warns especially those individuals who harbor such rage against others so that they would gladly kill them. Therefore, they must blot out their anger, for they know not how angry God will be at their judgment.

Part II of Fifth Commandment

Daz ander gebraeche ist: dû solt gein nieman keinen toetlîchen haz tragen unde nît.

b. Hatred and Envy

To bear deadly hatred and envy against an individual is to have murdered him in one's heart. Therefore people must eradicate these sins from their hearts; and, irrespective of whatever sorrow might have been caused, they must forgive the guilty, so that God in turn will forgive them.

Affirmatively, this precept commands to preserve our own lives and the lives of those whose temporal care is committed to us. Negatively, it forbids unjust killing, wounding, mutilation, striking, and also anger, hatred and revenge, the latter three sins because they lead to violence, injustice, and murder itself.

By Natural Law, man enjoys the use not the dominion of his life. He neither gave it nor may he take it away.[12]

The Sixth Commandment

Part I

The sixth commandment enlarges upon only one of its two sections. The first: *dû ensolt niht unkiusche sîn, dû solt niemannes lîp ze unkiusche begern, zer unê.*

a. Impurity

In a despairing tone, the preacher ejaculates " Oh, God! how many souls there are condemned every day for the violation of

[11] Cf. I 92, 3 ff.   [12] Cf. Davis, *op. cit.*, 113.

this sacred edict." Berthold then discloses that the prevalence of
lust in his day has robbed his contemporaries of all sense of
modesty and shame; impurity has become so habitual that they
are even in danger of the punishment of Sodom and Gomorrha.
He decries the fact that very few show any shame for the guilt
of this sin; the greater number boast of committing sins of impurity which God has hated since the beginning of the world, and
which He has so often avenged. The people are reminded that
twenty-four thousand persons were slain at one time because of
impurity. If one were to die with this sin upon his soul, he must
suffer the tortures of hell-fire for even a momentary pleasure. The
whole world would strenuously repudiate the pain he would be
forced to endure.

1. *Adultery*

Berthold assures the congregation that adultery is one of the
greatest sins in the world because God has merely lent a consort
to the individual to whom one must remain true both in body and
soul. Neither married party has absolute right over his or her
body. Any infraction in this regard is a serious sin of injustice
toward the innocent party. Nevertheless, many of the married go
and hide away in stalls, and commit the disgraceful sin which act
they could legitimately perform with their consorts without disgrace and sin, but honorably *an einem schoenen bette*. Besides
bearing the guilt of breaking a sacred commandment, they sin
against one of the noblest Sacraments [13] which Christ instituted.[14]

Married persons must not seek excuses which they deem would
license them to commit adultery:

. . . der ein lebendigez gemechede hât, ist daz jenhalp mers oder swâ ez in
aller der werlte ist: die wîle ez lebet, sô maht dû niemer kein anderz
genemen. Ez sî gevangen . . . daz dû halt westet, daz ez dîn ougen niemer mêre gesaehen, dû möhtest doch kein anderz genemen, die wîle und
daz ez lebet, ez sî krump oder gereht, siech oder gesunt.   (I 316, 25 ff.)

Even though she be leprous, a woman may never grant her husband permission to take another wife, however good it would seem
for both, and for the issue:

[13] Cf. I 305 ff.; II 92 f. for Berthold's treatment of the Sacrament of
Matrimony.
[14] Cf. I 205, 37 ff.

Sê ûzsetziger! welich der tiuvel hât dir den gewalt gegeben oder verlihen,
daz dû im ein ander erloubest? jâ möhte daz der bâbest niht getuon. Oder
welich der tiuvel hât dich ze eime bâbeste gemachet? (I 316, 30 ff.)

Should this husband become mentally depressed and find it difficult to lead a chaste life, deprived of marital relations, he has two
alternatives: he may steal into the *hiuselin* to his leprous wife, or
he may become an adulterer, which, however, will damn his soul.[15]
Married people who have sexual relations with others are highly
cherished by the devil. They must never be *ungetriuwe an dem libe*,
because thereby they break the promise which they made to each
other before God to be loyal unto death. A violation of this vow
imposes two-fold punishment which the guilty must suffer.[16]
Were a person to avoid adultery simply out of fear of his natural
just reward, according to Berthold, he should be sent to the eternal
flames. It is a thousand times better to shun sin out of fear of
God, and the glory of His almighty power.[17] Therefore, one who
desires to commit adultery, and does not banish the desire out of
love for God, but because of fear that the husband might gain
knowledge thereof apd slay the unjust intruder, he deserves this
punishment if he sins with her. Or, if a woman does not yield to
the desire because of the physical punishment she might invite
(*durch villen unde durch schern*), then she deserves whatever may
befall her should she consent.[18]
Berthold warns against the evil which results from *gesiht der
unkiusche*:

Swer eine frouwen an siht in dem willen, daz er gerne mit ir sliefe, der
hât diu werc vollebrâht, und dâ von sol man sich hüeten. . . .
(II 139, 19 ff.)

Part II of Sixth Commandment

The second section of the sixth commandment: *daz ist ein sô
getâniu unkiusche, dâ von eht niemanne ze reden ist.*[19]* *Dâ be-
schirme uns der almehtige got vor und alle sîne heiligen!*

---

[15] Cf. I 317, 1 ff.
[16] Cf. II 189, 34 ff. Speaking elsewhere on the punishment imposed upon
adulterers, Berthold warns them of the *zwelfer leie marter*. Cf. II 190, 31.
For the penances and physical punishment adulterers and other transgressors were given in earlier times, cf. the historical treatment by J. Schmitz,
Die Bussbücher und die Bussdisciplin der Kirche (Mainz, 1883), *passim*.
[17] Cf. I 557, 32 ff.   [18] Cf. *ibid.*, 25 ff.   [19] Cf. II 218, 32 ff.

2. *Sodomy*

One of the four sins that cry to heaven for vengeance is so sinful, atrocious, harmful, and disgraceful, that no one can give it a name; it is, and will always be the world's worst sin.[20]   Though the devils have always been masters and devils of sins, even they have not dared seek and give a name to this *verfluocheste, verdampteste* sin.[21]   Satan himself could not name it, *sô gar verfluochet unde sô gar ungenaeme ist diu selbe sünde wider allen den sünden, die diu werlt ie gewan.*[22]   Berthold says further that the *verfluocheste* sin in question has many designations, but neither human beings nor devils could ever give it its right name.   In the vernacular, the sin is referred to as *diu rote sünde.*[23]

Pfech pfech! Sie heizet diu stumme sünde. . . . Daz dû waenest daz ist ez, unde dannoch mêr alle sîniu glîhtrîde; ein schalkhaft herze verstêt mich vil wol.   (I 93, 5 ff.)

Berthold regrets that a person guilty of this sin should have ever been baptized.   His hand is not worthy of even touching a stick; and to touch bread is out of the question entirely.   He ought not even handle clothing, or touch the gallows.   Moreover, he is not worthy of laying a hand upon the most loathsome viper and toad.[24] Nor should the sodomite touch any clean object, nor wine, nor a glass, nor a dish, nor even the trough from which swine will take their food.[25]

The preacher stigmatizes the hypocrisy of those guilty of this sin.   He asserts that those in his audience addicted to this sin give the impression that they are so innocent, they would not even cloud the waters of a brook, but their actions in private are known better to no one but their master, the devil, with whom they are always in so close proximity.   Berthold commands these sinners

---

[20] Cf. I 92, 20 ff.   Of sodomy, St. Bernardine of Siena says: " Bis zu den Sternen stinkt diese Sünde, die überall in Toskana und in Italien herrscht. In Deutschland kennt man dieses Laster gar nicht, ebensowenig in Frankreich."   Cf. K. Hefele, *Der Hl. Bernhardin v. S.,* . . . 42.   St. Bernardine preached extensively in Germany.   His sermons were interpreted.   Cf. P. Schaff, *History of Christian Church* (New York, 1910), V, Part II, 228 f.

[21] Cf. I 92, 25 ff.; 206, 34; 35.

[22] Cf. I 206, 35 ff.   [24] Cf. *ibid.,* 7 ff.

[23] Cf. I293, 2 ff.   [25] Cf. I 207, 9 ff.

to immediate and strictest penances, otherwise they shall be condemned to the depths of hell. Even hell is tainted by their presence.[26] Berthold draws the attention of his auditors to the fact that in the territory where sodomy was first committed, all forms of vegetation became extinct. Grain, for instance, grows in this land, wine and fruit in another, but nothing which man can enjoy grows in that eternally cursed place.[27] Berthold expresses his happiness over the ignorance of this sin at least among some members of the congregation; so, in God's name, he forbids them to question him, for it is better that they remain in their state of ignorance. Unlike his usual method, the preacher says that priests should never question anyone about this sin; they are not to mention a single word about it. To the inquiry of what a person should do if he is guilty of this sin, Berthold answers: *selbe tete, selbe hete.* Then he does, however, supply some advice: the person is to think "in his heart" if he ever committed a sin, which, because of shame he never dared confess, perhaps that is the sin! He must never permit this sin to enter his heart; he must confess it, however great it is.[28] Without offering an explanation, Berthold states that this sin has eight divisions, some of which even the devil in hell is ashamed.[29]

Berthold implores again that the guilty earnestly beg God to free them from that state, and after a good confession, make a firm purpose of amendment, and accept the penance from a merciful God. The alternative is suffering in hell: first the soul, and after Judgment Day, both soul and body.[30]

3. Incest

Prior to Berthold's comparatively brief discussion upon this sin, he informs his auditors that although God curses all unchastity, He moreover curses four kinds of unchastity before all other types, with special curses. Because the preacher states he hopes very few guilty of these sins are in his presence, a voice from the congregation suggests that the topic be abandoned for there is evi-

[26] Cf. II 218, 34 ff.
[27] Cf. I 93, 12 ff.; 206, 38 ff.
[28] Cf. I 92, 29 ff.
[29] Cf. I 207, 6 ff.
[30] Cf. I 93, 19 ff.

dently no need to sermonize on this point. Nevertheless Berthold
feels it his duty, so he answers that while there may be only very
few persons guilty of this sin among the people, there are many in
other lands; and just as the castle protects the master, so must
Berthold protect Our Lord from these sinners and that they in
turn may amend, and avoid the just, horrible curse.[31]

The major portion of the treatment accorded this sin, namely.
incest, consists in the presentation of Berthold's rather free trans-
lations of the following Latin text:

I Maledictus qui dormit cum uxore patris sui et reuelat operimentum
lectus eius et dicit omnis populus amen.
II Maledictus qui dormit cum omni iumento et dicit omnis populus amen.
III Maledictus qui dormit cum uxore proximi sui et dicit omnis populus
amen.

He offers brief comment on the first and third of the three curses
cast upon the guilty, to the effect that the wicked persons should
immediately perform strict penances for their offenses, or suffer
in hell. In regard to the third, he implies scornfully that the
guilty have gained nothing from their lives on earth. Even if
they could have escaped being among the cursed, they would have
been already sufficiently damned in committing that sin with those
to whom they are not related.[32]

In another sermon, obviously to frighten young people to whom
he directs his statements, Berthold discusses the evils which arise
from unchastity, one of the devil's worst snares. He employs an
example of incest to point out the disastrous results of yielding to
the devil's temptation to commit sins of the flesh. Absalom, who
first surrendered to the devil's snare to sin with his own step-
mother, fell easy prey to pride. This led him to take another
kingdom against his father's will. Then, after the devil had
ensnared him with hatred and envy, he warred and fought with his
father because the latter resented his son's behavior with his own
wife.[33]

By the sixth commandment adultery alone is forbidden explicitly; but all thoughts, words and actions which are intended
to lead or which naturally lead to it, and all actions contrary to

[31] Cf. II 218, 3 ff.   [32] Cf. *ibid.*, 17 ff.   [33] Cf. I 412, 26 ff.

the orderly propagation of the race are implicitly forbidden—
immodesty, divers venereo-sensual pleasures, etc.
Sins of impurity are consummated or non-consummated. The
consummated are commonly referred to as six in number: fornication, adultery, incest, criminal assault, rape and sacrilege. Non-
consummated acts of impurity are found in immodest touches,
looks, thoughts, talks, reading, which will be mortally sinful whenever they are indulged in with a view to exciting venereal pleasure.
Berthold does not discuss the latter here.

Besides being a grave sin against chastity, adultery is also a
serious violation of justice which prescribes fidelity to the marriage
vows as long as they exist. Even if the other party whose marriage
rights are violated by adultery should have given his consent to the
sin, it is still against justice, for, like the right to life, marriage
rights are inalienable, and cannot be renounced by those who own
them.[34]

The Seventh Commandment

Part I

The first section of the seventh divine injunction *dû solt niht
steln,* is *dû solt niemannes guotes ze unrehte gern, weder mit roube
noch mit diepheit noch mit wuocher noch mit fürkoufe noch mit
satzunge.*

a. Unjust Power

All persons who oppress others through unjust power are guilty
of one of the four sins that cry to heaven for vengeance—sins
which condemn one both in body and soul. Pharaoh who oppressed
the Israelites, lost his body and soul in the sea, and all his fol-
lowers met with the same end. Alexander, too, was damned. His
life was shortened and *er nam einen stinkenden tôt: er stank an
sînem ende daz nieman bî im mohte.* Berthold adds that the same
also happened to many others. By reason of their injustice, very
few *hôhen herren* attain old age and have good deaths. Their injus-

---

[34] Cf. Slater, *Manual of Mor. Theol.,* I 324-329, *passim.* For a good
theological treatment of incest, and " De peccatis consummatis contra
naturam," cf. *op. cit.,* 328 f.; 330-334; St. Thomas Aquinas, IIa IIae q. 64,
a. 5.

tice lies in depriving one of his honor, property, and body. They
tyrannize over individuals whom God created just as He created
them, to His own image and likeness, with body and soul, and
whom He redeemed just as He redeemed them.[35]

b. *Withholding Due Wages*

Both *nidern* and *hôhen* are exhorted to guard themselves against
this sin of injustice, which will make them cry to heaven for
vengeance. No one must withhold the due earnings of others even
über naht . . . über irs herzen willen. As often as they have earned
something for their services, carpenters, smiths, shepherds with
staffs, or thrashers with flails, they must receive their due wages.
Otherwise, speaking of the worker, Berthold warns his hearers that
*sîn bluot unde sîn sweiz ruofent sâ zehant über dînen lîp . . . und
sêle.* This sin against justice lies in the fact that God created all
persons equal, and the auditors are assured that everyone on earth
is equal in the eyes of God.

Wande er als edel ist als dû und er dir als swaerlîche gedienet hât, sô
gaebest dû im vil billîche daz kleine lôn, daz er umbe dich verdienet hât;
wan swie gâhes dû ez im gibest, sô hâst dû im dannoch niht gelônet als
hôhe als in got geedelt hât.   (I 90, 27 ff.)

Berthold lauds the custom in some countries that one may sue for
his due wages, and if they are given begrudgingly, the defendant
must give the judge six shillings *ze buoze.*

The preacher instructs employers to be absolutely certain that
their laborers and servants get sufficient food. If they expect their
help to work hard all year, they must never be let go hungry.
Berthold laments the fact that instead of *grôze schüzzeln* for the
servant and laborer, the master often substitutes a *katzen vas*, or a
gnawed bone, which the employer ought to give to his own children,
or to his cats, or throw to his dogs. It is pitiable when servants are
commanded: *ezzet vaste!* The employer never means they should
eat at ease, and eat enough; it is the order that the workers are to
leave the table in a hurry, and leave whatever food is left, behind.[36]

[35] Cf. I 89, 13 ff.
[36] Cf. I 90, 7 ff.

c. *Theft*

In this division, Berthold concerns himself principally with the prevalence of deceitful, larcenous performances of merchants. They have become so calloused in their criminal habits, they have lost all sense of shame. With premeditated fraudulence, they give water for wine, they sell air for bread. The bread is inflated with yeast so much that the inside will be hollow. Instead of getting crumbs in the interior, one really buys an empty crust. Others sell pork for venison or unseasonable veal, from which a woman that has just been delivered, or a person whose blood has just been let, or a person suffering from any sickness when eating, may suffer ill effects and even death. Merchants also have false weights in their stores. They raise the scale on one side and turn it with their hands in such a way that it jolts the article, thereby deceiving the people. Despite his *wie sol ich dich trügenheit lêren? Sô kanst dû ir selber ze vil der trügenheit,* Berthold continues to warn people of these common crimes. Some vendors have false measures; others adulterate wax, and oil. Manufacturers of cloaks take useless old rags, which are so tattered one would not even think of throwing them on *eine want,* sew them together, starch the cloth, and sell that merchandise. Then they will sell it perhaps to some poor servant who has had to work six months for the price of the garment. He will get hardly a month's wear out of it, so that he is forced to purchase another one. Farmers, as well as merchants in the cities, are rebuked for their thievish ways. In every load of wood, they lay the crooked pieces in the center; they pack hay lightly, so in both instances they are selling nothing but air. Petty merchants alloy suet, and augment their crime by placing inferior apples and pears beneath the good ones. Millers, too, play an important rôle in deception and thievery. Laborers work efficiently as long as their supervisors backs are not turned. Shoemakers burn soles to make them appear heavy and durable, but they last scarcely a week.

Dû trügener! dû triugest manigen armen menschen, wan die rîchen getarst dû niht effen. (I 17, 13 ff:)

Tapsters contaminate good wine, which may cause a person to become deathly ill. By their thievery, tailors trick customers under their very eyes:

> wan er leget die gêren lang an den rok unde snîdet danne daz breite abe
> unden an dem gêren . . . sô hât er dirz gestoln, dû enweist hiute wie;
> unde sô dû waenest dû habest ein wîtez gewant, sô hâst dû sîn niht.
>
> (I 17, 28 ff.)

Furriers do likewise with imperfect pelts.

After he has obviously presented an adequate picture of the topic under discussion, Berthold repeats: *wie solte ich etelîchen diepheit lêren!* Some of their own kind are only too willing to instruct others in thievery. But they are warned that if they do not execute their commercial duties honestly, and give alms, they shall all be damned.[37]

Evidently Berthold is a firm believer in the maxim, " spare the rod and spoil the child."[38] He instructs parents that *gewonheit ist etewenne rîcher danne diu natûre,* so they must be vigilant; and whenever a child first learns to steal, *sâ zehant slahez mit einem rîse dar umbe.* Moreover, the child must never be released from the punishment, and he must be made to return the stolen article.[39]

Locusts know not where their shelter is at night; they are never warm, seldom eat well, and at all times live in fear of their lives. So it is with robbers, and thieves—the *boesen hiuten* who rob graves.[40] In another sermon Berthold states that thieves shall have a large shelter. Whether they steal much or little, whether they actually steal or do so by desire, they should go about with loud noise under the banner of *hern Achors* who stole until he was stoned to death.[41]

1. *Restitution*

Restitution must be made first by making amends to God to gain mercy, and secondly, to our neighbor according to justice. Berthold adds that the latter implies a three-fold duty: one must make amends to his neighbor, i. e. his fellow Christian, *genzlîchen, schiere,* and *froelîchen.* The preacher elucidates the points: " whatever injury you have done to your neighbor must be atoned for

---

[37] Cf. I 16, 8 ff., 17. Cf. I 478, 36 ff., 479.

[38] In several instances, Berthold makes references to this form of punishment to discipline children. Cf. I 35, 8 ff.; 33.

[39] Cf. I 35, 31 ff.   [40] Cf. I 230, 35 ff.   [41] Cf. I 261, 16 ff.

according to mercy." Restitution must be made by those guilty of all forms of injustice. They must repay down to the last farthing, otherwise they shall suffer eternal damnation. It must never be that, in order to spare the feelings of a child who has stolen,[42] a parent would gladly make restitution for the child with the help of Berthold who could be instrumental in requesting of the receiver that he accept only one-half or one-third of that which is to be returned. Berthold exclaims that neither the devil nor the Pope could help him. If the receiver were to approach the thief and ask him for one-half or one-third of that which was taken, and told the latter to keep the rest, the thief is even then not exempt from making full restitution—for the other would rather have complete restoration, as is just—for even while he is speaking, he is thinking " *mir ist bezzer ein wênic wan gar verlorn.*" If the thief does not want to make full restitution, and he sees that kindness is being shown him, he must take *gereitez guot*, as much as is to be restored, show it to the receiver and, without cunning, say: " *nû seht, diz guot bin ich iu schuldic: wellet ir mir daz widergeben, daz stê an iuwern gnâden.*" Whatever may be returned, may be justly kept.[43]

To the question asked by an auditor whether restitution may be extended over a period of four or five years—with Berthold's assistance—i. e., so the stolen goods could be returned a little at a time, the preacher answers forcefully in the negative: " *Sê, welich der tiuvel hât mir den gewalt gegeben über sîn guot?* " To make amends according to justice requires that restitution be made immediately. After it has been fully made, the guilty must ask pardon of the innocent person, for the goods that have been stolen may have caused him worry.[44]

Thirdly, then, *soltû im froelîchen büezen . . . froelîchen gelten unde widergeben*, so that he must not be forced to do so by the civil or ecclesiastical courts. At this point, the speaker is interrupted by a pessimist:

Pfî, bruoder Berhtolt! dû bredigest sô griulîche von unrehtem guote, daz ich vil nâhe verzwîvelt bin. (I 75, 30 ff.)

To this Berthold replies that God makes no difference between a big thief and a petty thief:

[42] Cf. II 102, 13 ff.   [43] Cf. I 73, 11 ff., 137, 4 ff.   [44] Cf. I 75, 14 ff.

Sich, daz waere mir vil leit, daz dû iemer deheinen zwîfel gewünnest . . .
hâst dû niht mêr unrehtes guotes wan aht pfenninge wert, unde dû weist
wol, wem dû sie gelten solt, unde wirst alsô funden daz dû ir niht giltest
und widergibest, dû muost alse lange in der helle brinnen, als got ein
herre in dem himelrîche ist.[45]   (I 75, 31 ff.)

Berthold terminates with a final plea to return stolen goods for
religious reasons:

Unde dâ von gewinnet alle samt wâren riuwen . . . unde gebet wider
durch die liebe unsers herren, daz ir iht ûzsetzic werdet von aller der
gemeinde, die diu heilige kristenheit hât, unde von . . . freude die die
heiligen in dem himelrîche habent, unde von der barmherzikeit . . . gotes.
. . .   (I 120, 14 ff.)

And, should an offender refuse to confess his sin and make restitution, his house ought to be torn down and he should be driven into
the fields. That is, of course, if he will not give up the ill-gotten
goods, and if he ignores the dictates of the ecclesiastical court.[46]

d. *Usury and Preëmption*

Among the ramifications of avarice, usury and preëmption create
the world's most monstrous sinners. They will scarcely be able to
stand final judgment, for they spend their time uselessly, disgrace-
fully, and sinfully. God Himself even spoke of them through His
prophets:

dû wuocherer unde fürköufer unde satzunger unde dingesgeber inz jâr . . .
dû rehter boese hût, dû laest mich niemer geruowen. Die von Sodomâ . . .
lant mich etewenne geruowen, aber dû . . . niemer. . . .
                                     (I 120, 16 ff., 25 ff.[47])

Since interest on loans was forbidden by the Church in the
Middle Ages,[48] Berthold vociferously condemns the vice, practiced
for the greater part by Jews. He entreats the wealthy to be
generous in making loans to the needy, for they will not become
poorer thereby; just as the sun that lends its light and warmth to
the whole world and does not become poorer, so too, the rich will
not become poorer. Therefore they must lend what God has merely
lent them. Frequently six pfennigs will help a poor person just

[45] Cf. I 259, 36 ff.
[46] Cf. I 122, 31 ff.   [47] Cf. II 130, 37 ff., 131, 1 ff., 236, 20 ff.
[48] Cf. Gärtner, *B. v. R. über die Zustände d. d. Volks*, 20.

as much if loaned to him as if given to him outright. But, Berthold warns, nothing must be taken in return—even an egg, or the cost thereof—for that would be usury. However, since the poor are, unfortunately, often corrupt, God, too, permits taking good securities on loans. Poor people tend to inconsistency and often break promises.[49] Another form of usury was credit. That which could be purchased for a reasonable price was, if bought on credit, raised to a tremendous amount.[50] It often happened that out of necessity a poor person took a measure of grain from an avaricious individual on credit, and instead of accepting the equal amount in return, the poor person was made to augment the lot one and a half times more. Poor people would have to work for nothing.[51] Berthold offers meagre material on preëmption. In most cases the numerous references to this vice occur casually. The preacher defines preëmption:

Daz ist: swenne dû. . . guot wilt an gewinnen oder an gewunnen hâst ze unrehter wîse . . . oder daz dû von ieman hâst gekoufet korn oder wîn, daz er dir aller êrste gap, dar nâch über ein ein help jâr oder über sehszehen wochen oder lanc oder kurz, unde dû im die pfenninge drûf gaebe, daz er dir ze nâhe gap, dan man ez mitten in die hant gap, unde swie vil des ist, daz dû deheinen kouf naeher hâst gekoufet: daz heizet fürkouf. . . .   (I 73, 20 ff.)

All ranks in the holy Priesthood are called upon to expose usurers and preëmptors. Laxity on their part to do so will have to be accounted for on Judgment Day.[52]

Part II of Seventh Commandment

The second division of the commandment under consideration is: *daz dû dîn reht gewunnen guot niht ze gîteclîche halten solt unde dû ez den armen liuten mite teilen solt.*

e. Social Charity

Once more Berthold enforces the necessity of faithfully executing the corporal works of mercy. Those who can, must always assist

---

[49] Cf. I 26, 23 ff.; 280, 39 ff.; 477, 6 ff.   [51] Cf. I 258, 3 ff.
[50] Cf. Gärtner, *op. cit.*, 21.   [52] Cf. II 2339, 6 ff.

8

the needy because they will be specially questioned on this matter on Judgment Day.

The preacher resumes his vehemence on the warning command that a donor must never become the recipient of any form of gift for his deed; or take interest on a loan which he has made. For the love of God and heaven, even if something is left on his doorstep, it must be returned, or he shall suffer eternally in hell. However, the receiver must always be certain to return the exact value of whatever may have been given him in loan. A person must never be put under pressure to speed the return of borrowed goods. If a poor individual brought back what he could, so that the donor would keep still, the former would live in constant fear he might be commanded to make complete return.

Unde sô in des dunket, sô bringet er dir eteswaz. Des soltû überein niht nemen, ez sî wîn . . . eiger, weder diz noch jenz. Dû weist vil wol, lihest dû im niht, daz er dir nihtes niht braehte. Dâ von solt dû sîn sus ouch niht nemen, oder dû bist ein rehter gesuocher.

The wide term *injustice*, according to Slater, may be used to designate any violation of justice, whether it be legal, distributive, or commutative. Sins against legal justice are committed by doing anything against the common good of society to which one belongs, or by neglecting to do what the common good requires to be performed. Such sins may be committed by rulers and subjects, more frequently however by the former, inasmuch as the common good is especially entrusted to their care and guardianship. Distributive justice prescribes that the ruler divide common burdens and emoluments among his subjects according to their merits and capacity. A ruler, who in his distribution of offices and burdens shows undue favor to some to the detriment of others, sins indeed against strict justice if he thereby cause damage to the community.

Of wages, St. James (v. 4) says that the employer's "great and principle duty is to give every one a fair wage." Doubtless before deciding whether wages are adequate, many things have to be considered; but wealthy owners and all masters of labor should be mindful of this, that to exercise pressure upon the indigent and the destitute for the sake of gain, and to gather one's profit out of the need of another, is condemned by all laws, human and divine.

devils! Be ashamed of yourselves. As you have been sinners and traitors, and the ancestors of all sins, you might well be ashamed of the fact that this baptized Christian has outwitted and surpassed you in sinning; it shall always be to your disgrace and shame that you do not dare commit a sin which a baptized Christian dare commit; for it would not do you much good. The preacher adds that he knows even the devil in hell would rather augment the pain which he is now suffering, than take such an oath.

Pfî, kristenmensche! sô lange sich der tiuvel schamen sol, sô mahtû dich des iemer schamen, daz dû die sünde getarst tuon, die der tiuvel ungerne taete.

Part II of Eighth Commandment

The second division of the eighth commandment is *lüge unde valscheit.*

b. Lies

Berthold discusses the eight kinds of lies according to St. Augustine.[56] He tells the congregation that of this number five are mortal, and three are venial. The first lie is, of course, the greatest; thereafter, the gravity decreases, so that the last in number is the least offensive.

The first lie is one against the Christian faith. For instance, if one were to say that God has never been tortured; or that the Blessed Mother is not a virgin; or whatever one might say that is similar to these lies. The second lie is to forfeit the life of another by lying. Those who fall under this category are referred to as *manslahter, menschenvrâz,* and *bluottrinker.*

Wie, menschenfrâz! jâ fraezest dû mir einen halben ohsen lieber an dem heiligen karfrîtage danne dû mir kristenmenschen verlügest.

The third lie is committed by dispossessing another of his honor. Berthold inquires of slanderers how they would feel if the same

Rechtsgeschichte (München und Leipzig, 1930), 22, 82, 178. Freidank, too, is vehement in his denunciation of existing law courts. Cf. Rapp, *Burgher and Peasant,* 66 f.

[56] St. Augustine, *De Mendacio,* c. 14.

To defraud any one of wages that are his due is a crime which cries to the avenging anger of heaven.

Theft is not only the secret taking away of what belongs to another, but also the keeping of it against his reasonable wish. The sin of theft is of itself grievous because it violates the great virtues of justice and charity. With regard to other delinquencies, their guilt may often be venial. The determination of what is grave matter has offered room for widespread difference of opinion. In his treatment of the seventh commandment, we see that Berthold is particularly the sociologist.

In the internal forum of conscience it is sufficient to indemnify the injured person for the injury which he has suffered, and in whatever way this is done conscience will be satisfied. Restitution then may be made by one's self or through another, with or without the knowledge of the injured party, under the guise of a gift, or by extra work in case of a servant, or greater diligence than is otherwise of strict obligation. If the form of a gift or present is chosen, and the donee makes a present in return, this may not be accepted if the principal motive for making it was to make a return for the present received, otherwise it may be retained when the receiving of the present was rather the occasion than the cause of the return being made.

Restitution must be made as soon as possible, and the unjust possessor of another's property will be responsible for all loss arising from even inculpable delay, as far as such loss could be foreseen. He became responsible for such loss when he took unjust possession of his neighbor's property. He must, at his own expense, take means to put the owner in possession of his property again.[53]

Money considered as a medium of exchange is a fungible; it is a commodity whose use is exhausted for the owner of it when he has paid it in exchange for value received. Money may be the matter of a contract of loan for consumption, and, if a sum of money be thus lent, justice requires that an equal sum be returned at the end of the term, and justice will not allow a greater sum to be exacted in return. For the whole value of the sum of money is the value it has for making exchanges, the value which it has in the first expenditure of it; and if, over and above the sum lent,

[53] Cf. Slater, *op. cit.,* 386-436, *passim.*

a further sum were demanded for the use of the money, the same thing would be charged for twice over. An equal sum is due in return for the use of the money; a further sum would be a second payment for the same use. Thus when money is regarded merely as a medium of exchange a sin against justice is committed if an additional sum besides the principal is exacted for a loan; it is called the sin of usury, money unduly exacted for the use of money. This is the reasoning of St. Thomas (IIa IIae q. 78, a. 1). By this argument he defended the doctrine concerning usury which the Fathers and Doctors drew from Holy Scripture and tradition.[54]

The Eight Commandment

Part I

Dû solt niht valsch geziuc sîn is the eighth commandment. This commandment belongs to the second, and like the other commandments has two parts, the first of which is: *daz dû durch liebe noch durch leit noch durch miete noch durch dekein dinc dînen valschen geziuc ûf niemanne füeren solt, wan daz ist der aller groesten sünden einiu, der wizzentlîche einen meineit swert, die diu werlt ie gewan.*

a. Perjury

Berthold speaks directly to perjurers, and commands them to listen to his explanation of the meaning behind the evil, superstitious manner they employ when giving false testimony. Perjurers perform identically as a thief who once stood before the judge and said:

seht, her rihter! als waerlîche als ich diz guot verstoln hân, als waerlîche sult ir mich dort hin ûz hâhen an den galgen. . . .

Perjurers always raise three fingers and lower two when taking an oath. They raise three fingers toward heaven to call upon God to witness the truth to what they are saying; yet at the same time they know in their hearts they are telling gross untruths. Berthold informs them that the first of the three raised fingers shows that they scorn God's mercy, and they have already pronounced judg-

[54] Cf. *ibid.*, 514 f.

ment upon themselves. With the second finger they renounce the assistance and intercession of the Blessed Mother who is the mediatrix for all Christians; but, by such evil action, no longer may they ever expect help from her. With the third finger they exclude themselves from the Communion of Saints; for, although they said that God and the saints assisted them in telling the truth while they were taking the oath, nevertheless, inwardly they knew they were lying. For this, neither God nor saint will ever listen to their prayers; they have condemned themselves; they will be damned by God and His saints. By lowering two fingers, Berthold explains, perjurers are pointing, with one, directly to the devil who also cast himself from God by falsities; in addition, they are showing God the direction in which He must send them after death. With the second finger they point to the society of all damned.

However, when a person takes an oath truthfully for himself or for a fellow-Christian, to what he saw and heard, the oath is a blessing. But, some say (turning to the *Eideshelfer*):

gevater (oder swie er danne wil), hilf mir mit einem eide, und wizze, ist sicherlîchen wâr: wes ich swere, des maht dû ouch wol sweren, ich naeme dehein guot, daz ich swüere ihtes, ez waere danne wâr.

The auditors are warned that if they take an oath under such circumstances they are committing perjury, for a person must swear only to what he himself has seen and heard. He must not surmise and take for granted that the other party is telling the truth. Furthermore, even if the latter person whom you are assisting in the oath is telling the truth, the Eideshelfer is nevertheless a perjurer.[55] Berthold rebukes these conjurors:—You devils, y

[55] Here Berthold condemns an established method of court procedure prevalent for centuries in German Law: conjuration. The defendant, upon whom the burden of proof usually rested, was allowed to exculpate himself from the complaint by an oath which he took either by himself, or with a certain number of *Eidhelfern*. The *Eidhelfer* swore that the defendant's oath was not perjurous (rein und unmein). Consequently these *Eidhelfer did not* testify as eye witnesses, but they testified that the defendant's oath was true; which, however, they could not generally verify by their own personal knowledge. Cf. H. Brunner, *Grundzüge der deutschen*

were done to them, and he tells them that their offense, in part, is even worse than avarice. Priests are told to give all sinners, excluding the avaricious and slanderers, penance according to their contrition. Mercy is not to be shown to avarice and to slander; neither in reliance upon God, His generosity nor kindness, but only according to justice. By justice Berthold says he means that the avaricious must repay to the last farthing if he can afford to do so; the liar must never be absolved unless he retracts every false statement he has made about his neighbor. Should many people in the parish have knowledge of this untruth, he must do public penance on Sunday before the entire congregation. Berthold tells the people that this act of repentance is indeed difficult to perform, and, in this sense, slander is worse than avarice; it is less difficult to repent after committing the sin of covetousness, than slander. At that moment if, among the audience, an avaricious person rose and said he would make complete restitution—it would be an honor for him. It would be an honor for the liar, too, if he would only realize it; it is always better for the liar to suffer shame in the presence of a few people, which will do him good, than have to be ashamed of himself before the whole world on Judgment Day when it will do him no good.

The fourth lie is to take another's property by lying. There are many guilty of this vice. Some are traitors and liars and go to their masters or to strangers and say:

'seht nû gît der wol zehen pfunt, ir sult in vâhen,' sô er lîhte niht vieriu hât.

Thus, some are deceivers and liars; just like so many merchants that are deceivers and liars. Many a shoemaker will display two rather good soles; but beforehand, he had burned them to change the appearance. In this way he lies and deceives for others' property. Similarly, the storekeeper who weighs food on imperfect scales; the baker who inflates the dough with yeast; in reality, he sells air for bread; the peddler who adulterates oil by pouring beer or water into it. There are butchers who tell customers the veal is three weeks old, and it is scarcely a week old; or he may sell putrid pork, from which a sick man or a woman who has just given birth may die. They are all deceivers and liars, and unless they make complete restitution for their sins, they shall be condemned.

The fifth lie is to rebuke a person who is to be praised, and when one praises a person who is to be rebuked, as the jester or minstrel. All of the above lies are mortal sins. Of the three venial sins, the first is if one wanted to take property belonging to another, and the latter asked you if you knew anything about it, and your reply was negative. The second lie is: if a man, who wanted to rob a maiden of her virginity, asked you if you knew her, and your reply was negative. The third is: if a person who wanted to kill a man whom his enemies were seeking, and although you did know of his whereabouts after they had asked you, but your reply was negative.

In the present day, the eighth commandment is not ordinarily combined with the second as Berthold does. However, he is not incorrect:—the second commandment prohibits unlawful oaths; the eighth prescribes the telling of truth; it forbids the giving of false evidence especially in a court of justice.

A lie is defined by St. Thomas (IIa IIae q. 110, a. 1) to be a speech contrary to one's mind. It is then the essence of a lie that there should be an intention of saying what is false, that there should be a contradiction between the mind and the external expression of it.

Lies are divided by theologians into jocose, officious, and hurtful lies. According to common Catholic teaching, lying of every kind is intrinsically wrong; so that, inasmuch as we may not do evil that good may come of it, we are never justified in telling a lie, not even if the life of another or the safety of the world depended upon it. St. Augustine, St. Thomas, and other Catholic Doctors and theologians gather this doctrine from the teaching of Holy Scripture, which in many places seems to forbid all lying as absolutely as it forbids theft or homicide (Col. iii. 9; Eph. iv. 25).

Lying is the perversion of the moral order which the law of nature prescribes should be observed between the mind and the expression of it in our intercourse with others; right order requires that the external expression should agree with the internal thought.

Mental reservations are either strictly or widely so called. The former is the restriction of one's meaning in making an assertion to the proposition as modified by some addition made to it within the speaker's mind. In wide mental reservations the words used are capable of being understood in a different sense, either because they are ambiguous in themselves, or because they have a special sense derived from the circumstances of time, place, or person in which they are spoken. Although strict mental reservations are lies, and therefore, sinful, yet wide mental mental reservations are in common use; they are necessary, because justice and charity require that secrets should be kept; they are not lies, because words take their meaning not only from their grammatical signification but from the circumstances in which they were used. Wide mental reservations must not be employed without just cause.[57]

Before proceeding to the ninth and tenth commandments, attention is drawn to Berthold's inversion of the order of these two commandments. The ordinary enumeration is reversed: he places the ninth commandment, "Thou shalt not covet thy neighbor's wife," last, and the tenth, in ninth place.

During the Middle Ages recitation of the Decalogue, "nach der biblischen Reihenfolge," was not always used.[58] Göbl analyses the enumeration of several ecclesiastical writers before Berthold's time, to show that the ordinary order of the Decalogue was often changed.[59]

The Ninth Commandment

Part I

The first subdivision of the ninth commandment *dû solt dînes ebenkristen dinges ze unrehte niht gern* is: *daz dû dînes ebenkristen guotes niht begern solt, daz dû dir iht gedenkest: ' owê! haet ich dem alsô vil oder alsô vil verstoln oder geroubet oder erlogen oder ertrogen!' Daz gebot hoeret ûf daz sibende.*

Berthold accords the ninth commandment special treatment. Like the other precepts he subdivides this commandment into two parts; however, he offers no material on the second division. Desire is discussed meagerly in the first section only.

a. Covetousness: Desire of Neighbor's Goods

A voice from the audience inquires of Berthold why a person would lose his soul if he had not executed his desire to steal or

[57] Cf. Slater, *op. cit.*, 464 ff.
[58] Cf. Göbl, *op. cit.*, 170.   [59] Cf. *ibid.*, 171 ff.

obtain something by fraud.   Berthold answers that if he would like
to have gained another's property unjustly, and was prevented
from carrying out his plan for no reason other than that it was
impossible, then he must remember that God will judge him only
as He sees him in his heart; and God knows every thought he has
had and ever will have, both good and bad.   The preacher continues to say that his hearers must believe that God can see into
hearts.   After all, God created the heart and placed it into every
body, so He, better than everyone else, knows what goes on in it.

Part II of Ninth Commandment

The second division is: *daz dû ez versuochest mit allem dînem
flîze unde dich dar nâch arbeitest, wie dû einem sîn guot verstelst
unde geroubest oder mit andern untriuwen an gewinnest, unde daz
niht für sich gêt.   Wirdest dû in dem willen funden, sich, dû muost
êwiclîche verdampt sîn.*

The Tenth Commandment

Part I

The tenth commandment *dû solt dînes ebenkristen gemechede
niht begern* has the first part: *swer eine frouwen in dem willen
unde in der andâht ane siht, daz er gerne sünde mit ir taete, der
hât diu werk vor gote vollebrâht.*

Covetousness: Desire of Neighbor's Wife

a. Culpability of Men

Berthold acknowledges an utterance from one among the auditors
that, because of this injunction, scarcely one man will be saved.
The preacher then offers his explanation: if a person found a thief
in his cellar who had broken a box, but had removed none of its
contents, the former would indeed consider him a thief and have
him brought to the scaffold.   Likewise God considers an individual
a real adulterer, for in case he is not really such externally, he is a
thief, quite properly in that part.

Part II of Tenth Commandment

The subdivision is: *dû solt niht gern, daz man dîn gere.*

b. Culpability of Women

In the first part, Berthold says that men are condemned to eternal fire; in the second part, the women are damned, for they prepare and make themselves up for the devil's snare, and,

ist daz sich nieman drin ervellet, doch müezent sie daz gerihte haben unde tragen unde daz urteil des lebendigen gotes.

Such is the snake that has a *megetlîche houbet,* carries hidden pus, and is ever ready to inject the poison with which she will kill a soul: her dancing eyes, her treacherous gait, her mask, and her clever manner. Therewith she draws away chastity from a soul.

It is written in the Old Testament: "If a man has dug a well in the road, and a neighbor's cow falls in, he must reimburse him. If he does not cover the well, then he must reimburse him for the cow with the price at which it was bought, and the cadaver belongs to him who did not cover the well and who must reimburse for the cow." Berthold tells the people to note well that the carcass belongs to him. All who make themselves up and prepare themselves to incite others to sinful things in thought or in deed, and they do not cover their own sins, so that they sin without restraint, and openly, and do not cover the well of their sins, they give scandal to others, and set bad example. Furthermore, the preacher tells the guilty people: all whom you bring into mortal sin by this bad picture, by scandal, and with your *reizekloben,* those you must reimburse to Almighty God with the same price as He bought them, and the cadaver remains yours. God bought them through His passion; and you have abducted and led them astray from Him into eternal death; at such price you must reimburse Him for them, or you will be damned to eternal torture, and the cadaver remains with you. These are all those who go to hell through your fault; all of them are thrown upon you, so that you have to suffer all their pain in addition to your own. Berthold concludes by saying that it is easily understood how one gets the carcass.

FINAL REMARKS

Conclusion of this study may be made with a final observation on the question whether Berthold von Regensburg can be considered a predecessor of Luther. The picture of moral life in the thirteenth century which Berthold creates and develops for us, with vigorous emphasis on the negative tendencies and qualities of all classes of people, shows how he fought against existing conditions with an utmost conservatism and an almost unrelenting severity. The corrective measures which he proposes are inspired solely by a sincere intention of arousing humanity against prevailing sins, and re-establishing ideal conditions in the Christian world as they existed in the cradle days of Christianity. But the mere fact that, at times, he unreservedly impeaches evil members of the clergy, and that now and then he makes a remark which may be interpreted as conformable with Luther's theology, should not have furnished the reason for E. W. Keil to arrive at one definite conclusion from his study, namely, that Berthold is to be classified as a forerunner of the sixteenth century Religious Revolution. For the purpose of ᷍ ᷍ dissertation, "Religious Revolution" means the overthrow on the part of Luther, of the existing doctrinal, moral, and ecclesiastical system and teachings of the medieval Church.

However forcefully Berthold rebuked the faults and vices of certain individual members of the clergy, he never displayed any hostility toward the Church or the clergy as such. He loved the Church and its teachings, and thought that there was no chance for salvation outside her fold. There exists no justification for the slightest doubt that Berthold lacked a profound faith. He saw society through the Church, hence he never deviated from the view which religion suggested. He saw God, His Blessed Mother, and the Saints in everything; he saw all things in their supernatural relations. Berthold possessed the greatest horror for sin, and for him the reform of the world meant simply the reform of the sinner.

Although Berthold makes derogatory comments on the Pope, still he was a firm believer in the institution of the Papacy. He regarded the spiritual power of the Pope, and of all priests, as more important than the Emperor and Kings. Since the preacher made it his task to attack evil, no matter where it was found, he had to be consistent and direct his attacks against all guilty of wrong-doing, including even the Pope. Berthold staunchly believed in the infallibility of the Pope, but did not claim impeccability for the incumbent of Peter's Chair.

Practices of the Church which Berthold in contrast to Protestantism stresses are, for example, the Sacrifice of the Mass, and confession, and good works. Berthold held fast to the Sacrament of Penance of which confession is an integral element, differing in this regard from Luther.

Hence, Berthold preached a reform only in the sense of urging a return to moral life on the part of the clergy and laymen, but it never occurred to him to overthrow the time-honored and sacred institutions of his Church. Dr. Keil might be justified in claiming Berthold to be a forerunner of the Religious Revolution; but in one sense only, namely, if he has in mind that Berthold as a critic of existing conditions of his time, excoriated abuses which undoubtedly did exist both among the clergy and laity. But Keil in this regard has added not one iota to our information, for even conservative historians have again and again admitted the necessity of personal moral reform, but not of dogmatic reform. Objectively, then, Berthold von Regensburg is an earnest, convinced and faithful Catholic character, and hence he can never be called a forerunner of the Religious Revolution.

A summary of Berthold's treatment of the capital sins and of the decalogue is in place here. As has already been mentioned in this work, Berthold discussed all the capital sins but only in a spasmodic and unmethodical manner. When he speaks of avarice, for example, he is apt to confuse because the slightest reference of one sin immediately leads him to lapse into the discussion of another.

In his discussion of pride, he dwells for the greatest part on the utter absurdity of elaborate garments. Rich and poor, young and old receive violent reproaches. Among these classes, women, especially, are warned frequently that if they do not thwart pride they are forfeiting their eternal salvation. The wealthy, too, will be condemned because by their arrogance they victimize the poor. Pride will likewise cause the poor loss of eternal happiness because this vice leads them to nurse an inordinate desire for power and honor. The young gain a sinful air of superiority through pride.

Throughout all his sermons, the most frequently mentioned vice is avarice. Berthold regards it as the most harmful and the world's worst evil. It is one of the capital sins which he discusses detailedly and with most vehemence. One of his complaints against the avaricious is the iniquitous manner in which they waste their God-given time. He reminds them often that they are certain to be condemned to the depths of hell. Unequal distribution of goods, unjustly acquired property, and hoarding are considered ways of serving the devil. Old persons particularly seem prone to this sin since they can no longer participate in dancing, they cannot quarrel, commit unchaste deeds, or go about with pride. Children are cautioned to repudiate ill-gotten goods inherited from their parents. The covetous person murders his own soul and the souls of those who become heirs to his unjust gains. In confession, priests must insist that the guilty make complete restitution before they can receive Absolution. Concerning avaricious persons, the preacher makes an interesting analogy: he says they are like grasshoppers— they have a coat of armor, human-like countenances, women's hair, lion's teeth, and a scorpion's tail. They form an entire company with Judas as the manager.

In his discussion of lust, Berthold levels censures primarily against the young, because they are easily addicted to this sin. The preacher suggests repeatedly that the young marry and not live like cattle. Parents are instructed to supervise their children even in church because it happens often that the House of God is used by procurers to pervert young people. Berthold rebukes the notion entertained by many that fornication is not as sinful as the priests make it out to be. He exhorts the layman against committing any unchaste act with a religious for this sin will condemn the guilty to the eternal fires of hell. Berthold adds that he would rather die without receiving Holy Communion than to assist at Mass in the same church with a person who has sinned with a religious; and he would rather not hear Mass if he knew that the celebrant had ever yielded to the temptations of the flesh.

Gluttony is frequently associated with unchastity, and Berthold attributes the former to an inordinate love of body which causes thousands of souls to be damned. Gluttons sit and eat to such excess that their stomachs expand four times their normal size. Gluttony is so injurious to the body that the evil effects are indescribable. He goes on to explain, however, that if a kettle in which food is being cooked is filled too much, the contents become uncontrollable; they must boil over. The food does not cook, and at the same time it will burn. It must be remembered, he says, that the liver lies next to the stomach and supplies great heat which boils food in the stomach. If a person is not frugal in his eating habits he will become ill. Gluttony likewise produces consumption or recurring fevers. Few children of the rich reach adulthood because they are surfeited. On the Last Day gluttons will be dragged into the depths of hell. Where references to this vice are made, the poor are reminded that no statements are directed to them.

Hatred and envy are referred to as "apprentices of the devil." Berthold suggests that the devil garner those who are hateful and envious because they are misfits in the Kingdom of God. Those, who out of hatred and envy, begrudge their friends property gained by honest work or good fortune, will be denied help by the saints who will inflict wounds upon them that will never heal. Hatred and envy engender murder, robbery, and incendiarism.

Anger is one of the causes of all sins. The person who inclines to anger is as bitter as gall which transforms persons into murderers, robbers, traitors, and slanderers. Many murder their wives through anger. It it not uncommon that men beat their wives beyond recovery. Anger leads some to commit the sins that cry to heaven for vengeance. Poor people for the most part are condemned for this sin; the elite are ashamed to resort to the coarse demeanor induced by anger. God does not want those who out of anger curse, rage, swear, or gnash their teeth, or those who fling whatever happens to be close by, or those who tear into shreds their own clothing or that of their wives.

All classes of society are reproached for their slothfulness. Many will go to hell because they are too lazy to go to church, or to say one Our Father. They demonstrate sloth in their service of God, and yet manifest eagerness for sensual pleasure, story-telling, and fatuous conduct. Some persons would not go to church if it were not that people would talk. Christians are exhorted to say sixty or seventy Our Fathers a day. All who reach the age of fourteen years and die without knowing the Lord's Prayer are to be buried in the potter's field. Berthold laments that the slothful should have ever been born. Parents who are indolent in rearing their children shall be guilty for all the misdeeds the latter perform.

Berthold's own enumeration and arrangement of the Decalogue embrace all the sins, whether of omission or commission, of which a man in the Middle Ages might be guilty. Like the seven capital vices, the Ten Commandments are also presented in an unsystematic and digressive manner although each precept is divided into two parts.

In his discussion of the first commandment, the preacher directs the majority of his vehement invectives to peasants and to women. The vicious practices of women, he says, are enough to make a man lose his mind. Women would cast spells to win the affection of a man. Furthermore, they are rebuked for their sorcerous bewitchings: women think they execute charms by using toads, wild apples, the Sacred Host, and Holy Oils. These persons are told they are the devil's chosen people who will be rewarded with a place of honor in the depths of hell. Only one remark in this section is made on idolatry. The second division of this commandment deals with an injunction which would receive scant consideration today. The people are instructed never to allow their thoughts to dwell on matters of Faith, for Faith is like the sun to which no one can direct his gaze without becoming blinded. Likewise may no one "direct his gaze" to the Christian Faith, lest his Faith become "ill." The treatment given heresy deals with the nefarious machinations of the guilty, and Berthold's preoccupation of familiarizing the people therewith so that they may be instructed into ways of safeguarding their Faith. He says heretics appear as priests who speak sweet, convincing words; they will speak of God, and Angels. The simple of heart and mind are especially warned to be on guard against those who will tell them that mortal sin is non-existent, and that marital privileges may never be enjoyed after either husband or wife has had the occasion of receiving Extreme Unction. Monastic greed is blamed for the prevalence of sacrilege and simony.

In elaborating on the second commandment, no distinction is made between profane language, cursing, and swearing. In Berthold's opinion each of these faults alienates the guilty from God. Heretics, gamblers, merchants, and women are made objects of the preacher's attacks. Parents are warned against regarding the bad words uttered by their offspring as an indication of precociousness. The third precept occasions Berthold to exhort the populace how not to spend Sundays. People must neither travel about nor require their servants to work; they must not conduct themselves boisterously, indulge in unchaste actions, play dice, or dance. Immediately after assisting at Mass, they are to return home and rest. Sins committed on any week-day afflict Our Lord mightily. On Sundays the magnitude of the offense is enormous. The holier the day, e. g., Easter or Pentecost, the greater the pain caused Our Lord. Individuals who work in the fields on Sundays will never enjoy their harvest. They will languish in sickness, and the profit gained from the crops will be lost through theft, fire, or hail. A typical instance of Berthold's discursiveness and repition takes place in the second section of the third commandment. With this precept he links the seven capital vices. It is noteworthy that only once is reference made to the obligation of assisting at Mass on Sundays.

The obligation of honoring parents and clerics is discussed in the fourth commandment. Children will be denied entrance into God's Kindgom if ever they had scorned or had been ashamed of their parents because they were poor, ill, deformed, or unattractive. Priests, because of their sublime office, must be tendered reverential respect at all times; they are to be honored by word and deed. The duties of parents are not mentioned.

A violation of the fifth commandment is one of the worst crimes known to mankind. Anyone refusing to obey the command to feed the hungry is a murderer. Avarice and anger are again introduced and Berthold shows how they lead to murder. Even the desire to commit murder will condemn a soul. " Blood-drinkers " are asked if the world has become wanting in beer, water, and wine, that they should see fit to spill human blood and devour human flesh.

The treatment of the sixth commandment alludes to the rampancy of lust in Berthold's time. So many, he says, have become hardened to this sin; they feel no sense of shame; they boast of their impurity. Once twenty-four thousand persons were slain because of impurity. The tortures of hell-fire that the guilty must endure after death defie description. The congregation is told that many married persons hide away in stalls and furtively commit

9

adultery. Married people are rebuked for seeking excuses to commit adultery. Even though she be leperous, a woman may never grant that her husband take another wife. Should this husband become mentally depressed and find it difficult to lead a chaste life, he has two alternatives: he may steal into the hospital to his leperous wife, or he may indulge in adultery which, however, will damn his soul. Adulterers are cherished by the devil. If a man desires to commit adultery and does not banish the desire out of love for God, but because his paramour's husband might apprehend him, he will be condemned to eternal flames. Sodomy, says Berthold, is the world's worst sin. Even the devil has not dared give it a proper name. Berthold regrets that those guilty of this sin should have ever been baptized. He is unworthy of touching the most loathsome toad and viper, nor any clean object, nor a glass, nor a dish. The Sodomite is ever in close proximity with the devil; yet he gives the impression that he is innocent. In Sodom where the sin was first committed all forms of vegetation have become extinct. Berthold expresses his happiness over the ignorance of this sin among some members of the congregation. Berthold states that this sin has eight different divisions of which the devil himself is ashamed. The divisions are not named. A voice from the audience suggests that the topic of incest be abandoned for there is evidently no need to sermonize on that point. But Berthold feels it his duty and answers that while there may be only very few persons guilty of this sin among the people in his presence, there are many in other lands. Berthold commands the incestuous to perform the strictest of penances.

In the seventh commandment unjust power receives scant treatment. All persons who oppress others through unjust power will be condemned in soul, and after Judgment Day, both in soul and in body will they be punished. The preacher instructs employers to be absolutely certain that their laborers and servants get sufficient food and their due wages. He lauds the custom in some countries of suing for one's due wages. Concerning theft, Berthold preaches against the prevalence of deceitful, larcenous deeds of merchants. With premeditated fraudulence they sell water for wine, inflate bread with yeast to such an extent that one really gets an empty crust, they sell pork for venison from which a woman that has just been delivered or another sick person may suffer ill effects or even death. Merchants use false weights. Wax and oil are adulterated. Cloth is made from old rags. Farmers, too, have thievish ways: they lay crooked pieces in the center of a load of wood; they pack hay lightly. Petty merchants alloy suet. Shoemakers burn soles to make them appear heavy and durable. Parents are warned not to spare the rod and spoil the child who steals; they must be vigilant and when a child first learns to steal he must be punished. Restitution must be made completely and immediately by those guilty of injustice. Partial restitution will not be condoned. Usury and preëmption create the world's most monstrous sinners. Since interest on loans was forbidden by the Church in the Middle Ages, Berthold condemns this vice, practiced for the most part by the Jews. A donor must never become the recipient of a gift in any form. Berthold expounds on the necessity of executing the Corporal Works of Mercy.

Perjurers are reminded that they will suffer harshly for nonobservance of the eighth commandment. When taking false oaths, perjurers have the custom of raising three fingers and lowering two. The first of the three fingers shows that they scorn God's mercy and have already pronounced judgment upon themselves. With the second finger they renounce the intercession of the Blessed Virgin. With the third finger they exclude themselves from the Communion of Saints. For such actions they will be damned by God and His Saints. One of the two lower fingers points directly to the devil; and the other points to the society of the damned. Berthold informs *Eideshelfer* that they are perjurers. (Here Berthold condemned an established method of court procedure prevalent for centuries in German Law: conjuration.) There are, according to Berthold, eight kinds of lies. The first is one against the Christian Faith. The second is the forfeit of the life of another through a lie. The third is the dispossession of another's honor. The fourth is the taking of another's property by lying. The fifth is the rebuking a person deserving of praise, and the lauding one who is to be rebuked. These lies are mortal sins. The remaining three kinds of lies are venial sins.

Attention is drawn to Berthold's inversion of the ninth and tenth commandments. The ordinary enumeration is reversed. During the Middle Ages, this often happened. Like other commandments,

Berthold subdivides the ninth commandment into two parts, but he offers material only on the first section.

In the ninth commandment, Berthold explains that a person would lose his soul even if he had not executed his desire to steal. The audience is told that an individual is judged only by God's looking into his heart.

The mere desire for another's wife, or the desire for another's husband is, in the sight of God, adultery. The guilty one is like a snake that carries hidden venom and is ever ready to inject the poison with which a soul will be killed. A covetous woman draws chastity away from a soul with her dancing eyes, treacherous gait, alluring mask, and voluptuous manner.

A retrospect in the study at hand indicates that Berthold was, above all, a mighty preacher to his people. There are many evidences of his true piety, conviction, and a sincere desire to save and teach all men. Obviously, he is far removed from the intention of preaching for his own fame and reward; he preached for the glory of God and the help of his fellow-Christian. Repentance was his principal theme. Berthold powerfully and unflinchingly attacked the sins of all classes; he was no respector of persons whenever he found abuse, whether among laity or clergy.[1] He satirized and denounced the sinful follies of polite society and the baser vices of all orders; in fact, he scorned sinners of every hue. On the other hand, he painted in glowing colors the beauty of Christian virtues, and the present and eternal rewards of the Christian life. Berthold was wonderfully gifted in the art of fresh, vivid, moving popular address. Invective, warning, appeal, exhortation, all were at his command. However homely and sometimes coarse his imagery and illustration, Berthold's dialogue was vivid and certainly sufficiently clear to quicken and guide the spiritual life of his auditors. It is also noteworthy that Berthold is given to the use of superlatives quite freely, forgetting the implication of the respective gravity of the different vices in relation to one another, and the respective nobility of the virtues in their interrelation. Berthold was, of course, a *medieval* didacticist. His thoughts, therefore, were concentrated on the life beyond death. Life before

---

[1] Cf. also H. Dargan, *A History of Preaching* (New York, 1905), 258 f.

death was a prelude to heaven or hell. It was the Hereafter that gave reality and meaning to life on earth. With Judgment Day ever uppermost in his mind, Berthold strove to convert the sinner by exhorting the sinner how *not* to live so that he would avoid eternal Punishment, and gain Paradise. Berthold was indefatigable in his attempts to crush vice in all classes of society by proving that everything temporal is futile and that a solid Faith and firm adherence to God's Commandments is the only sublimation that assists man in attaining perfect peace on earth, and heaven after death. His negative approach—a good weapon for instilling fear into the unequipped minds of his hearers by portraying the horror of the loss of the Beatific Vision—and his simplicity evidence Berthold's sincerity of purpose and his anxiety to instruct his auditors to think logically, and to employ common sense. Situations must always be carefully weighed; one must never supply his natural wants, or satisfy one's impulsive tendencies unless they conform to the Will of God.

BIBLIOGRAPHY

I. SPECIAL WORKS

Bernhardt, E., *Bruder Berthold von Regensburg*, Ein Beitrag zur Kirchen-
Sitten- und Literaturgeschichte Deutschlands im 13. Jahrhundert,
Erfurt, 1905.

Bihl, M., "Ein unediertes Leben Bruder Berthold's von Regensburg,"
Historisches Jahrbuch, 29 (1908), 590 ff.

Bouman, A., "De Zinsbouw van Berthold von Regensburg's Predigten,"
Neophilologus, 5 (1921), 218-30; 309-15.

Coulton, G., "A Revivalist of Six Centuries Ago," *The North American
Review*, CLXXXVI (1907), 274 ff.

Fassbender, F., *Die Stellung des Verbums in den Predigten des Berthold von
Regensburg*, Diss., Bonn, 1908.

Föste, K., *Zur Theologie des Berthold von Regensburg*, Programm Zwickau,
1890.

Gärtner, T., *Berthold von Regensburg über die Zustände des deutschen
Volks im 13. Jahrhundert*, Programm Zittau, 1890.

Geiger, O., "Studien über Bruder Berthold, sein Leben und seine deutschen
Werke," *Freiburger Diözesanarchiv*, 48, 1-54.

Gildemeister, H., *Das deutsche Volksleben im XIII. Jahrhundert nach den
deutschen Predigten*, Diss., Jena, 1889.

Göbel, F., *Die Predigten des Franziskaners Berthold von Regensburg*,
Regensburg, 1929.

Greeven, H., *Die Predigtweise des Franziskaners Berthold von Regensburg*,
Programm Rheydt, 1892.

Greiff, B., *Berthold von Regensburg in seiner Wirksamkeit in Augsburg*,
Programm Augsburg, 1865.

Grimm, J., *Kleinere Schriften*, Bd. IV, Berlin (1869), 296 ff.

Hoffmann, C., "Neue Zeugnisse über Berthold von Regensburg," *Münch.
SB.* (1867), 2, 3, 378-94.

Keil, E., *Deutsche Sitte und Sittlichkeit im 13. Jahrhundert nach den
damaligen deutschen Predigern*, Dresden A., 1931.

Kjederqvist, K., *Untersuchungen über den Gebrauch des Konjunktivs bei
Berthold von Regensburg*, Lund, 1896.

Kling, C., *Bruder Berthold's Predigten*, Berlin, 1824.

Kock, O., *Die Bibelzitate in den Predigten Bertholds von Regensburg*, Diss.,
Greifswald, 1909.

Kohn, M., "Berthold von Regensburg ein Sozialethiker des Mittelalters,"
Wochenschrift Deutschland (1890), Nr. 26-28.

Lebsanft, A., *Die religiösen und ethischen Ausdrücke bei Berthold von
Regensburg*, Diss., Tübingen, 1923.

117

118   *Bibliography*

Leitzmann, A., " Zu Berthold von Regensburg," *Zeitschrift für deutsches Altertum*, Bd. 54, 279-84 (1910-11).

Mertens, H., *Die Form der deutschen Predigt bei Berthold von Regensburg*, Würzburg, 1936.

Nussbaum, E., *Metapher und Gleichnis bei Berthold von Regensburg*, Diss., Wien, 1902.

Paul, T., *Berthold von Regensburg und das bürgerliche Leben seiner Zeit*, Programm, Wien, 1896.

Pfeiffer, F., *Berthold von Regensburg—Predigten*, Vol. I, Wien, 1862; Vol. II, Pfeiffer—J. Strobl, Wien, 1880.

Piffl, R., *Einiges über Berthold von Regensburg, auf Grund seiner Predigten*, Programm, Prag, 1890.

Rehorn, K., " Die Chronistengeschichte über Bruder Berthold's Leben," *Germania*, 26, 317-38.

Rieder, K., *Das Leben Bertholds von Regensburg*, Diss., Freiburg i. B., 1901.

———, *Der sogennante St. Georgener Prediger aus der Freiburger und der Karlsruher Handschrift*, Berlin, 1908.

Roetteken, H., " Der zusammengesetzte Satz bei Berthold von Regensburg," *Quellen und Forschungen zur Sprach- und Kulturgeschichte der germanischen Völker*, 53 (1885).

Schönbach, A., *Studien zur Geschichte der altdeutschen Predigt*, 8 Stücke, in 1 vol., Wien, 1900-07. Also in *Sitzungsberichte der Wiener Akademie*, vols. 140; 142; 147; 151; 152; 153; 154; 155.

Scheinert, M., *Der Franziskaner Berthold von Regensburg als Lehrer und Erzieher des Volkes*, Diss., Leipzig, 1896.

Schleich, R., *Der Humor in den Predigten Bertholds von Regensburg*, Programm Weisskirchen, 1892.

Schmidt, J., *Über Berthold von Regensburg*, Programm, Wien, 1871.

Schweizer, B., *Berthold von Regensburg—die vier Stricke des Teufels*. Bruchstück einer bisher unbekannten Pergamenthandschrift der Predigten Bertholds von Regensburg († 1272). Diessen a. A., 1922.

Sokol, A., " Das Grundproblem der Gesellschaft im Spiegel Bertholds von Regensburg," *The Germanic Review*, XI (1936), 147-163.

Steinmeyer, R., " Berthold von Regensburg," *Realencyclopädie für protestantische Theologie*, III (1896), 649-52.

Stromberger, C., *Berthold von Regensburg der grösste Volksredner des deutschen Mittelalters*, Gütersloh, 1877.

Toifel, O., *Über einige besondere Arten der Satzstellung bei Berthold von Regensburg*, Programm Ried, 1900-01.

Unkel, K., *Berthold von Regensburg*, Köln, 1882.

Wackernagel, W., " Bruder Berthold und Albertus Magus," *Zeitschrift für deutsches Altertum*, 4, 575 f.

Wieser, T., *Bruder Berthold von Regensburg, eine Kulturbild aus der Zeit d. Interregnums*. Programm Brixen, 1889.

II. GENERAL WORKS

Adams, G., *Civilization During the Middle Ages*, New York, 1894.

Aertyns, J., *Theologia moralis secundum doctrinam S. Alfonsi de Liguorio*, 2 vols., Paderbornae, 1906.

Aguirre, J. S. de, *De virtutibus et vitiis disputationes ethicae*, Romae, 1697.

Aquinas, St. Thomas, *Opera Omnia*, Parisiis, 1871-1880.

———, *The Commandments of God*, trans. by L. Shapcote, O. P., London, 1937.

Albert, R., *Die Geschichte der Predigt in Deutschland bis Luther*, Gütersloh, 1896.

Aumann, E., " Tugend und Laster im Althochdeutschen," *P. B. B.* (Vol. 63 (1/2), 1939 (pp. 143-161).

Baentsch, B., *Das Bundesbuch*, Halle, 1893.

Baldwin, S., *The Organization of the Medieval Christianity*, New York, 1929.

Bartsch, K., " Die Formen des geselligen Lebens im Mittelalter " (*Gesammelte Vorträge und Aufsätze* (Freiburg und Tübingen, 1883), 221-249.

Batten, L., " Decalogue," *Encyclopedia of Religion and Ethics*, IV, 513 ff.

Beer, M., *Social Struggles in the Middle Ages*, London, 1924.

Behrendt, L., *The Ethical Teaching of Hugo of Trimberg*, Diss., Washington, 1926.

Bernhart, J., " Vom Geistesleben des Mittelalters. Ein Literaturbericht," *Deutsche Vierteljahrschrift für Literaturwissenschaft und Geistesgeschichte*, 5 (1927), 172-212.

Bezold, F. v., *Aus Mittelalter und Renaissance* (Ch. II), München u. Berlin, 1918.

Billot, L., *Disquisitio de natura et ratione peccati personalis etc.*, Romae, 1897.

Bisle, M., *Die öffentliche Armenpflege der Reichsstadt Augsburg. Ein Beitrag zur christlichen Kulturgeschichte*, Paderborn, 1904.

Boehn, M. von, *Die Mode: Menschen und Moden im Mittelalter vom Untergang der alten Welt bis zur Renaissance, nach Bildern und Kunstwerken der Zeit ausgewählt und geschildert*, München, 1925.

Boissonade, P., *Life and Work in Medieval Europe (Fifth to Fifteenth Centuries)*. Trans. by Eileen Power, London, 1927.

Brandi, K., *Mittelalterliche Weltanschauung, Humanismus und nationale Bildung*, München, 1923.

Brown, W., *The Achievement of the Middle Ages*, London, 1928.

Bühler, J., *Das deutsche Geistesleben im Mittelalter*, Leipzig, 1927.

———, *Die Kultur des Mittelalters*, Leipzig, 1931.

Cathrein, S. J., V., *Die katholische Moral*, Freiburg i. B., 1907.

Cheney, C., *Episcopal Visitation of Monasteries in the Thirteenth Century*, Manchester (Univ. Press), 1931.

Clemen, C., *Die christliche Lehre von der Sünde*, Göttingen, 1897.

Coulton, G., *Life in the Middle Ages*, 4 vols. in I, New York, 1930.

Cruel, R., *Geschichte der deutschen Predigt im Mittelalter*, Detmold, 1879.

Dargan, H., *A History of Preaching*, New York, 1905.

Dieffenbacher, J., *Deutsches Leben im 12. und 13. Jahrhundert*, vol. I, Öffentliches Leben (Smlg. Göschen, Leipzig, 1919); vol. II, Privatleben, Leipzig, 1907.

Döllinger, J., *Heidenthum und Judenthum*, Regensburg, 1857.

Dresdner, A., *Kultur und Sittengeschichte der italienischen Geistlichkeit im 10. und 11. Jahrhundert*, Breslau, 1890.

Dubois, S. M., E., *Saint Francis of Assisi Social Reformer*, Diss., Washington, 1904.

Ehrhard, A., *Das Mittelalter und seine kirchliche Entwicklung*, München, 1908.

Ehrismann, G., *Geschichte der deutschen Literatur bis zum Ausgang des Mittelalters*, Erster Teil, 2. Aufl. (München, 1932); Zweiter Teil, I (1922); Zweiter Teil, II (1927); Zweiter Teil, Schlussband, 1935.

Eicken, H. v., *Geschichte und System der mittelalterlichen Weltanschauung*, 4th ed., Stuttgart und Berlin, 1923.

Erdmann, K., *Die Entstehung des Kreuzzugsgedankens*, Stuttgart, 1935.

Farrar, F., *The Voice from Sinai*, London, 1892.

Feret, P., *La faculté de théologie de Paris. Moyen âge*, 4 vols., Paris 1894-1897.

Francke, K., *Die Kulturwerte der deutschen Literatur des Mittelalters*, 2nd ed., Berlin, 1925.

Franz, A., *Drei deutsche Minoritenprediger aus dem XIII. und XIV. Jahrhundert*, Freiburg i. B., 1907.

————, *Die Messe im deutschen Mittelalter*, Freiburg i. B., 1902.

Frassinetti, G., *Compendio della theologia morale*, 2 vols., Genoa, 1866.

Freytag, G., *Bilder aus der deutschen Vergangenheit*, Bd. I (Insel-Ausgabe), Leipzig, 1926.

Friederich, J., *Kirchengeschichte Deutschlands*, 2 Bde., Bamberg, 1867.

Funk, F., *Zins und Wucher. Eine moraltheologische Abhandlung*, Tübingen, 1868.

Galtier, S. J., R., *Le péche et la pénitence*, Paris, 1929.

Göbl, P., *Geschichte der Katechese im Abendlande vom Verfalle des Katechumenats bis zum Ende des Mittelalters*, Kempten, 1880.

Götting, F., *Der Renner Hugos von Trimberg*, Münster i. W., 1932.

Goetz, Sr. M. P., *The Concept of Nobility in German Didactic Literature of the Thirteenth Century*, Diss., Washington, 1935.

Grabmann, M., *Mittelalterliches Geistesleben; Abhandlungen zur Geschichte der Scholastik und Mystik*, 2 Bde., München, 1926-1936.

Grieshaber, F., *Deutsche Predigten des 13. Jahrhunderts*, 2 Abt. Stuttgart, 1844-1846.

Grundmann, H., *Religiöse Bewegungen im Mittelalter; Untersuchungen*

Bibliography

über die geschichtlichen Zusammenhänge zwischen der Ketzerei, den Bettelorden, und der religiösen Frauenbewegung im 12. und 13. Jahrhundert und über die geschichtlichen Grundlagen der deutschen Mystik, Berlin, 1935.

Grupp, G., *Kulturgeschichte des Mittelalters*, 6 vols. Paderborn, 1907-1925.

Grayzel, S., *The Church and the Jews in the Thirteenth Century*. Philadelphia, 1933.

Harnack, A., *Das Wesen des Christentums*, Leipzig, 1901.

Hasak, V., *Der christliche Glaube des deutschen Volkes beim Schluss des Mittelalters*, Regensburg, 1868.

Haskins, C., " The Spread of Ideas in the Middle Ages," *Speculum* 1 (1926), 19-30.

Haw, G., *Christianity and the Working Classes*, New York, 1906.

Hefele, C. J. v., *Conciliengeschichte* (nach Quellen bearbeitet), vol. V, 2nd ed. by A. Knöpfler, Freiburg i. B., 1886.

Hefele, H., *Die Bettelorden und das religiöse Volksleben Ober- und Mittelitaliens im XIII Jahrhundert*. Diss., Tübingen. Leipzig, 1910.

Hentsch, A., *De la littérature didactique du moyen âge*, Diss., Halle, 1903.

Hemelt, T., *Final Moral Virtues in Sociology*, Diss., Washington, 1929.

Höfler, C. von, *Die romanische Welt und ihr Verhältnis zu den Reformideen des Mittelalters*, Wien, 1878.

Huizinga, J., *Herbst des Mittelalters*. Studien über Lebens- und Geistesformen des 14. und 15. Jahrhunderts in Frankreich und in den Niederlanden, 3. Aufl., deutsch von T. Wolff-Mönckeberg, München, 1931.

Hulme, E., *The Middle Ages*, New York, 1929.

Joyce, G., *Christian Marriage*: an historical and doctrinal study, London and New York, 1933.

Koch, A., *A Handbook of Moral Theology*, adapted and edited by A. Preuss. 5 vols., 2nd ed. 1919-1924.

Köster, A. und Petersen, J., *Geschichte der deutschen Literatur*, Bd. I von H. Schneider, Heidelberg, 1925.

Kraetzschmar, R., *Die Bundesvorstellung im A. T.*, Marburg, 1896.

Kriegk, G., *Deutsches Bürgertum im Mittelalter*, N. F., Frankfurt, 1871.

Lamprecht, K., *Deutsches Wirtschaftsleben im Mittelalter*, 3 vols., Leipzig, 1885-86.

Lecoy de la Marche, *La chaire française au moyen âge*, éd. 2, Paris, 1886.

Lefranc, A., *La vie quotidienne au temps de la renaissance*, Paris, 1938.

Lemme, L., *Die religionsgeschichtliche Bedeutung des Dekalogs*, Breslau, 1800.

Leyser, H., *Deutsche Predigten des XIII und XIV Jahrhunderts*, Quedlinburg, 1838.

Liguori, St. Alphonsus M., *The History of Heresies, and their Refutation*, Trans. by Rt. Rev. Dr. Mullock, Dublin, 1857.

Linsenmayer, G., *Geschichte der Predigt in Deutschland von Karl d. Gr. bis zum Ausgang des 14. Jahrhunderts*, München, 1886.

122   *Bibliography*

Limmer, R., *Bildungszustände und Bildungsideen des 13. Jahrhunderts*, München, 1928.

Lortz, J., *History of the Church*, Trans. and adapted from the 4th German edition by E. Kaiser, Milwaukee, 1938.

Loserth, J., *Geschichte des späteren Mittelalters von 1197 bis 1492*, München, 1903.

Macculloch, J., *Medieval Faith and Fable*, Boston, 1932.

Martin, A. v., " *Das Problem der mittelalterlichen Weltanschauung*," *Deutsche Vierteljahrschrift für Literaturwissenschaft und Geistesgeschichte*, 3 (1925), 485-500.

Mausbach, J., *Die Ethik des heiligen Augustinus*, 2. Aufl., 2 Bde., Freiburg i. B., 1929.

———, *Katholische Moraltheologie*, Bd. II, Münster i. W., 1921.

———, *Die katholische Moral und ihre Gegner*, Köln, 1913.

Meisner, O., *Der Dekalog*, Halle, 1893.

Michael, S. J., E., *Geschichte des deutschen Volkes seit dem dreizehnten Jahrhundert bis zum Ausgang des Mittelalters*, 6 Bde., Freiburg i. B.

Migne, L'Abbé, *Dictionnaire de philosophie et de théologie scolastiques au moyen âge*, Paris, 1865. (In Encyclopedie théologique vols. 21-22.)

Mignon, A. l'Abbé. *Les origines de la scolastique et Hugues de Saint-Victor*, 2 vols., Paris, 1895.

Müller, E., *Theologia Moralis*, 3 vols., Vindobonae, 1873.

McDoniugh, M., *The Chief Source of Sin*, Baltimore, 1910.

Neander, A., *Über die Eintheilung der Tugenden bei Thomas Aquinas*, Berlin, 1847.

Neumann, M., *Geschichte des Wuchers in Deutschland bis zur Begründung der heutigen Zinsgesetze*, Halle, 1856.

Nikel, G., *Allgemeine Kulturgeschichte*, Paderborn, 1895.

Noldin, H., *Summa theologiae moralis*, 3 vols., Oeniponte, 1908.

Owst, G., *Preaching in Medieval England*, Cambridge, 1926.

Peters, N., *Die älteste Abschrift der zehn Gebote*, Freiburg i. B., 1905.

Robinson, G., *The Decalogue and Criticism*, Chicago, 1899.

Romain, G., *Le moyen âge fut-il une époque de ténèbres et de servitude?* Paris, no date.

Roth, K., *Deutsche Predigten des XII. und XIII. Jahrhunderts* (in Bibliotek der gesammten deutschen National-Literatur, Elften Bandes erster Teil) Quedlinburg u. Leipzig, 1839.

Shahan, T., *The Middle Ages, Sketches and Fragments*, New York, 1904.

Schaub, F., *Der Kampf gegen den Zinswucher, ungerechten Preis und unlauteren Handel im Mittelalter*, Freiburg i. B., 1905.

Schulze, P., *Die Entwicklung der Hauptlaster und Haupttugenden von Gregor dem Grossen bis Petrus Lombardus und ihr Einfluss auf die frühdeutsche Literatur*, Diss., Greifswald, 1914.

Scherer, W., *Geschichte der deutschen Literatur*, 14th ed., Berlin, 1921.

Schnürer, G., *Kirche und Kultur im Mittelalter*, 3 vols., Paderborn, 1924-29.

Scherr, J., *Deutsche Kultur- und Sittengeschichte*, 3 vols., Leipzig, 1909.

Schönbach, A., *Altdeutsche Predigten*, 3 Bde., Graz, 1886-1891.

Schröder, E., " Die Summe der Tugenden und Laster," *Zeitschrift für deutsches Altertum*, 29 (1885), 357-360.

Schulte, A., *Der Adel und die deutsche Kirche im Mittelalter*, Stuttgart, 1910.

Schwane, J., *Allgemeine Moraltheologie*, Freiburg, 1885.

Sedgwick, H., *Italy in the Thirteenth Century*, 2 vols. in 1, Boston and New York, 1933.

Singer, S., *Mittelalter und Renaissance* (Sprache und Dichtung II, Tübingen, 1910), 1-28.

———, " Der Geist des Mittelalters," *Germanisch-Romanische Monatsschrift*, 17 (1929), 81-96.

Slater, S. J., T., *A Manual of Moral Theology*, 3 vols., New York and Chicago, 1907-1908.

Stone, S., *The Seven Capital Sins*, Milwaukee, 1926.

Steinhausen, G., *Geschichte der deutschen Kultur*, Leipzig u. Wien, 1913.

Taylor, H., *The Medieval Mind*, 2 vols., 4th ed., London, 1930.

Tocco, F., *L'Eresia nel medio evo*, Firenze, 1884.

Troeltsch, E., *Augustin, die christliche Antike und das Mittelalter*, München und Berlin, 1915.

———, *Die Soziallehren der christlichen Kirchen und Gruppen*, 2nd ed., Tübingen, 1919.

Tupper, F., " The Medieval Husband," *The Sewanee Review*, XXVII (1919), 330-342.

———, *Types of Society in Medieval Literature*, New York, 1926.

Turmel, J., *The Latin Church in the Middle Ages*. Trans. by A. Alexander, New York, 1915.

Vernet, F., *La spiritualité médiévale*, Paris, 1928.

Vetter, F., " Lehrhafte Litteratur des 14. u. 15. Jahrhunderts," *Deutsche Nationalliteratur*, XII.

Waddell, H., *The Wandering Scholars*, 7th ed. London, 1934.

Walsh, J., *The Thirteenth Greatest of Centuries*, 4th ed. New York, 1912.

Weinhold, K., *Die deutschen Frauen in dem Mittelalter*, 2 Bde. Wien, 1897.

Weiss, B., *Das Buch Exodus*, Graz, 1911.

Wellhausen, J., *Die Composition des Hexateuchs und der historischen Bücher des Alten Testaments*, Berlin, 1889.

Welter, J., *L'Exemplum dans la littérature religieuse et didactique du moyen âge*, Paris et Toulouse, 1927.

Zoepfl, F., *Deutsche Kulturgeschichte*, 2 vols.; 2nd ed., Freiburg, 1931.

INDEX

Adolescents, 25, 33.
Adultery, xvi, 67, 84 f.
Agatha, Saint, 7.
Aged, The, xii.
Almsgiving, 20 ff., 46.
Alphonsus, Saint, 71.
Anegenge, Das, 4.
Angels, 11, 20, 51.
Anger, 46 ff., 83.
Animals, 69. 72.
Anthony of Padua, Saint, 4.
Arrogance, 11.
Augustine, Saint, 48, 72, 100.
Avarice, 4, 15 ff., 22, 74 f.

Babylonians, 58.
Babylonische Gefangenschaft, 4.
Bad Companions, 27.
Bakers, 101.
Baptism, 57, 67.
Bawds, 26.
Beatific Vision, 38, 59.
Beggars, xii.
Benedict, Saint, 4, 15.
Bernardine of Siena, Saint, 7, 86.
Blacksmiths, xi.
Blasphemy, 67 ff., 70 f.
Blessed Virgin Mary, 4, 14, 20, 26 f.,
    49, 68, 69.
Boasting, 12.
Butchers, 101.

Capital Sins, xvi, 1, 2, 4, 5.
Catherine, Saint, 27.
Cassian, 1.
Celibacy, xii.
Charity, xii, 12, 13, 20 f.
Chastity, 13, 26 ff.
Children, 9, 17, 25, 30, 35, 69, 75, 81.
Church, The, xii, 1, 21.

Civil and Ecclesiastical Courts, 61,
    68, 93.
Clergy, xii, 43, 80 f.
Cloisters, xi, 19, 23, 63.
Clothing, 7, 8, 12.
Cluniac Movement, 2.
Cluniac Monks, 15.
Communion of Saints, 99.
Confession, 19.
Consumption, 35.
Cornelius a Lapide, xiii.
Corruption, xii *passim.*
Country People, 30.
Covetousness, 103 f.
Credit, 95.
Criminals, xii.
Crusades, xii.
Cursing, 69.

dalmut, 62.
Das St. Trudperter hohe Lied, 4.
Dancing, 10, 12, 14, 16, 17, 72, 76.
David v. Augsburg, 15.
Death, 3, 11.
Debauchery, 37.
Decalogue, xvi, 54 f., 77, 103.
Devil, 17, 27, 43, 47.
Dice, 16, 51, 68, 72.
Die altdeutsche Genesis u. Exodus, 4.
Diligence, 51 ff.
Diseases, xii.
Drinking, 34, 76.

Eating, 34.
Egyptians, 58.
Elias, 37.
Esau, 33, 36.
Extreme Unction, 62.

Faith, xvi, 4, 13.

125

DATE DUE

DEC 02			
NOV 14			
APR 20			